THINK

Yourself

HAPPY

DON CLOWERS

Editing, cover design, and formatting by ChristianEditingandDesign.com

Contents

Contents

Introduction

We all deal with life experiences. As long as we live, we will have to decide how to handle the challenges that inevitably come our way. Those decisions will be based on how and what we think.

You may have experienced injustices, abuses, and other bad things that make life seem unfair. Let me settle that one for you: Life is not fair. God never promised anyone it would be. In fact, Jesus warned about the trials and hardships we would all face. He did not say He would remove them, but He promised to help us through them and even bring good from them.

The Bible clearly teaches that the way you choose to *think* is critical. You can either think about how unfair, unkind, or ugly a situation is and feel sorry for yourself or think about Jesus' promises to help you through it. You can live with fear and anxiety, or you can learn to find peace in every situation.

What you think about in the middle of trouble will determine the outcome. You get to choose. In *Think Yourself Happy*, I hope to help you learn the importance of your thinking and how to transform negative thoughts into positive ones, no matter what the circumstances. This is not a self-help book. It *is* a book to guide you to the help available from Jesus.

If you have never committed your life to Jesus Christ, you may wonder if these biblical principles apply to you. They are for everyone who decides to follow Him. I hope you will make that choice (more about how to do that in Chapter 10). Following Jesus doesn't mean you won't have problems—but it does mean you will never face them alone.

ARE YOU READY TO CHOOSE GOOD THOUGHTS?

If you are ready to think yourself happy, you must be willing to make a deliberate transformation in your thinking that will lead to healthier thoughts and feelings. It's not that easy to change, but if you want to, you can.

In this book I will show you how to recognize ways that negative thinking may be affecting your life. We will look at God's Word to see how thoughts that trigger bad habits, depression, and despair can be transformed into thoughts that help you find the happiness and victory God promises.

Chapter 1

God Wants You to Be Happy

God wants you to be happy. Are you?

You may not feel happy. Perhaps circumstances are causing you to worry, fear, or even experience anger.

In our own lives and ministry, my wife and I have faced betrayals, financial setbacks, the near-fatal accident of our six-year-old daughter, and the death of our fifteen-year-old son. Heartbreaks and calamity are common to us all, but the Bible makes it clear that God wants us to live happy, abundant lives.

So how does that work? The secret to overcoming every unpleasant issue in life lies in the way we choose to think. In this book, you will learn how to think positive thoughts and make good decisions that are based not on emotion but on the goodness of God and His promises.

Learning to navigate through unhappy circumstances has never been more important. In a culture of polarizing opinions, heightened emotions, and a shifting economy . . . in a time when right is called wrong and wrong is called right . . . many feel the world is coming apart. It is more important than ever for our minds to be transformed. For us to think according to the truths and promises of the Bible. Only then can we become victors and not victims. Only then can we think ourselves happy.

One of my favorite reminders from the Bible was written by the apostle Paul.

> *Finally, brethren, whatever things are true,*
> *whatever things are noble, whatever*
> *things are just, whatever things are pure, whatever*
> *things are lovely, whatever things are of good*
> *report, if there is any virtue and if there is anything*
> *praiseworthy—meditate [think] on these things.*
> PHILIPPIANS 4:8

This scripture provides clear, detailed guidelines about how we should *think* in every situation. Paul makes a passionate plea for us to think on good things, thus positioning ourselves to be overcomers in every area of our lives. Our thoughts transform into what we believe and, in turn, what we do and how we deal with the problems that come our way. My hope is that as you apply what you learn in this book, you will be able to think yourself happy.

AN EXAMPLE OF RIGHT THINKING

You may recall the story in the book of Acts where the apostle Paul stood trial before King Agrippa. I have read the story many times, but recently I saw something I had never noticed before.

The story goes like this. Paul was in prison. The many charges against him included insurrection for allegedly coming against the Jewish Law, the temple, and even Caesar himself. Paul was innocent of the trumped-up charges, none of which could be proved. But that did not stop two Roman governors, Felix and Festus, from unlawfully condemning him to prison.

At that point, Paul had a decision to make. He could fold under pressure and give in to his fate—or he could rise up and fight for justice. As a Jew, he knew his rights, but he had to choose how he would *think* about and respond to his situation. Instead of reacting in fear or anger to the biased decisions of these governors, Paul chose to go over their heads. As a Roman citizen, he filed an appeal to King Agrippa to have his case presented to the higher court of Caesar in Rome.

In the middle of an unpleasant situation, Paul chose how he would think, resulting in one of the greatest overturning of circumstances recorded in the Bible. Here's how it went:

> *Then Agrippa said to Paul, "You are permitted*
> *to speak for yourself." So Paul stretched out*
> *his hand and answered for himself: "I think*
> *myself happy, King Agrippa, because today I*
> *shall answer for myself before you concerning all*
> *the things of which I am accused by the Jews."*
> ACTS 26:1–2

"I think myself happy."

Paul did not allow the situation to dictate how he would think and feel; he *chose* to *think himself happy* despite the accusations of others and the prevailing circumstances. His feelings were governed by his *thinking*, not the conditions he faced. And his thinking was based on his faith in Jesus and the Bible.

YOU HAVE A CHOICE

What circumstances are affecting your thinking right now? A troubled relationship? Rebellious children? Illness? Finances? The chaos in the world around us?

How are you reacting to those things? Fear? Anger? Worry? Confusion?

Wrong thinking can produce all these reactions and more. In this book, I will share what I've learned about how wrong thinking can bring about stress and worry, fear, anxiety, guilt, unforgiveness, discontentment, and self-doubt—and hinder healing from loss, such as death and divorce. I will also share what the Bible says about overcoming all that by developing right thinking.

For as he thinks in his heart, so is he.
PROVERBS 23:7

Chapter 2

Fear and Anxiety

Fear and anxiety can be debilitating, and they can come from many sources.

Anxiety is a meteor shower of *what-ifs*. Anxiety and fear come from the same family, but they are not identical twins. Fear sees a threat, but anxiety imagines one.

Do you keep up with daily news headlines? They may stir up all kinds of emotions—including fear.

Will prices keep going up? How will I provide what my family needs?

I am afraid to send my children to school. I am reading about so many bad things children are being exposed to these days.

With all the shootings, I am afraid to go out in public . . . afraid even at home.

I am so afraid to go anywhere without wearing a mask.

And on and on . . .

Fear and anxiety can rear their ugly heads in response to our personal circumstances as well.

What if I get fired?

What if my spouse leaves me?

What if someone I love dies?

What if my child starts taking drugs?

The *what-if* list is endless.

A PERSONAL *WHAT-IF*

On a personal note, I experienced something very negative in my life many years ago. While I was out of town speaking at a meeting, my wife, Sharon, was home with our four children. One day our daughter, Tammy, was accidentally hit by a car, leaving her critically injured. My wife called me with the bad news, and the trauma of that moment was forever etched in my mind. Sharon urged me to get home as soon as possible. The doctors had informed her there was little to no hope Tammy would survive even long enough for me to make it back home. Since it would take time to get there, I had only one option—PRAY. I sought strength and courage for my wife and healing for my daughter.

I immediately booked my flight home, but it would be excruciating hours before I could arrive at the hospital. I knew I had to take control of the thoughts racing through my mind—thoughts that Tammy would be getting worse as I journeyed home. A sense of helplessness overwhelmed me.

Finally, I arrived at the hospital and headed straight to the intensive care unit where my daughter was being attended. The situation was much worse than I had anticipated. I was shocked and dismayed at Tammy's desperate condition and appearance. Because of the thoughts and emotions racing through my mind, it was all I could do to maintain some composure. I had to step up and get control of my emotions, especially for the sake of my wife. The hours of being with my daughter as her life was hanging in the balance had taken their toll on Sharon. She needed my encouragement. She needed me. And we both needed God.

I beseeched the Lord for His help. We needed His strength. Sharon and I stepped outside the room and began to pray. I had to grasp hold of His promises rather than what I had just seen. Soon, both of us began to feel His strength. His power became evident, and we had the strength to stand. Tammy's healing was a long process, but we chose to focus on her healing and God's promises rather than her present condition. Hope sustained us as we faithfully awaited the answers to our prayers.

The answers came, little by little. After Tammy was doing better, I began traveling again, ministering in churches and crusades, but something had happened inside me. Things began to bother me that had never bothered me before. The *what-ifs* consumed me. Whenever the phone rang, sudden thoughts of fear would loom large in my mind. When I was on the road, every time the phone in my hotel room would ring, the traumatic call about Tammy would replay again in my mind's eye—fear. What if the caller on the other end of the phone was waiting to deliver another dose of bad news? After several rings, I would finally answer, but a long silence would transpire before I could even muster up a hello.

One negative, horrific event had stirred up fear that wouldn't go away. Fear told me there was tragic news on the other end of that phone line. Those thoughts of fear were beginning to control me. Even though I received many calls that delivered great news, my thoughts always seemed to dwell on pure negativity.

Subconsciously, my mind had stored the pain of the past and caused me to experience fearful feelings, terrifying *what-ifs*. That terrible time was in the past, but my memory bank was replaying old feelings.

Finally, I decided I would not continue living like that—I had to take control rather than be controlled. I knew that changing my thinking and ridding myself of the thoughts that triggered fear were steps I must take to regain control of my life.

The phone could bring me good news as well as bad news. Truth be told, the phone calls almost always brought me good news. That one bad event was shaping a part of me, and if I didn't change, the fear would drain me of the peace God wanted me to have.

With God's help, I began to look at the phone and say aloud, "Phone, you do *not* frighten me. You bring me good news. God has not given me a spirit of fear, but of power, love, and a sound mind."

> *For God has not given us a spirit of fear, but*
> *of power and of love and of a sound mind.*
> 2 TIMOTHY 1:7

For a long time after that, whenever I was away from home and the phone rang in my hotel room, the feelings of fear still tried to lay hold of my mind. I would answer the call and quickly overcome the *what-if* fear. Ultimately, good feelings overtook the bad, and I have never again been bothered by the sound of a ringing phone.

Of course, I have received bad news on the phone at times since then, but the ringing of the phone is no longer accompanied by feelings of fear.

I had recognized the wrong thinking. I had made a choice to focus on Jesus and His promise of peace in the Bible. As my thinking became more positive, the fear gradually left me.

FREEDOM FROM FEAR

Let me ask you, what do you meditate on most? What are you pondering? What are you giving your attention to? What are you contemplating? Are any of these thoughts triggering fear in your life?

Think about this: Every outcome in your life was started with a thought you let dominate your thinking. When fear becomes the dominant force, you will not live in peace. Peace is so valuable. You should go to bed in peace, wake up in peace, and go about your day in peace. When I minister, I must have peace. When I am traveling, I must have peace. Peace makes life so much sweeter. How do I maintain my peace? I keep my mind set on the right things—which is easier said than done. But you *can* do it. Let me take you back to Isaiah 26:3 "You will keep him in perfect peace, whose mind is stayed on You, Because he trusts in you."

Why will we have peace? Let's start at the end of this scripture. What does it say to do? It says to trust Him. Okay, how am I going to trust Him? First, I get my mind set on Him. This verse tells me when my mind is set on Him, I will have peace.

When we rely on God, we make Him the priority in our thought life and actions, so that whatever comes, we acknowledge Him and His Word first. How can you get to that place of trust? Keep your mind fixed on Him and His Word in all situations. I trust in Jesus because my mind and attention are focused on Him.

> *Then you will experience God's peace,*
> *which exceeds anything we can understand.*
> *His peace will guard your hearts and*
> *minds as you live in Christ Jesus.*
> PHILIPPIANS 4:7 NLT

God will guard your heart and mind as you keep your eyes on Jesus and trust Him every day. This is the key.

When you are in traffic and someone cuts you off or gives you hand signals that you know are not very nice, do you keep your peace? Or do you get in their world and let them rob you of your peace? If you will keep your thought life right and fixed on Him, no one can take your peace from you.

God's promise stands firm; He will visit and pour out His Spirit on us. When our enemy, Satan, is raging in this world, God is still God, and His peace will prevail in our hearts when we trust Him no matter what is going on. We are in this world, but we are not of this world. Heaven is our final destination, so fear not what man can do to you.

> *"Do not fear [anything], for I am with you; Do*
> *not be afraid, for I am your God. I will strengthen*
> *you, be assured I will help you; I will certainly take*
> *hold of you with My righteous right hand [a hand*
> *of justice, of power, of victory, of salvation]."*
> ISAIAH 41:10 AMP

This scripture proclaims to you that there is nothing to fear because He is with you. He says He will strengthen and help you. If you find yourself sinking into fearful thoughts about your future, stop focusing on the fear and begin proclaiming the Word of God.

CURRENT EVENTS ARE NO SURPRISE TO GOD

Current events can instill fear in each of us. But they come as no surprise to God, and we can trust Him to see us through. For some time, we have been experiencing Bible prophecy coming to pass. The Bible speaks of earthquakes, floods, storms, famines, pestilence, wars, and nations rising up against nations before Jesus returns to earth. The world has never experienced times such as we see in this generation: calloused terrorists, suicide bombers who blow themselves up only to take the lives of others, countries and races and cultural and political groups attacking one another with such hatred. Jesus warned us that when we see such things happen, we are not to be troubled or afraid.

> *"But when you hear of wars and commotions, do not be terrified; for these things must come to pass first, but the end will not come immediately."*
> LUKE 21:9

Think about the events of the past several years alone. Traumatic things are happening now and getting worse every day. The increase in natural disasters. Terrorism. Building of hatred toward Israel. The pandemic. Famines. Good things called bad and bad things good. Walls of hatred and aggression among the people. Sexual and gender deviation we never thought possible.

> *But know this, that in the last days perilous times will come: For men will be lovers of themselves, lovers of money, boasters, proud,*

*blasphemers, disobedient to parents, unthankful,
unholy, unloving, unforgiving, slanderers,
without self-control, brutal, despisers of
good, traitors, headstrong, haughty, lovers
of pleasure rather than lovers of God, having
a form of godliness but denying its power.
And from such people turn away!*
2 TIMOTHY 3:1–5

Sound familiar?

But if you turn to Jesus, you do not have to live in fear.
Take comfort in His words:

*"These things I have spoken to you, that in
Me you may have peace. In the world
you will have tribulation; but be of good
cheer, I have overcome the world."*
JOHN 16:33

When you see terrible things happening in our world,
remember these encouraging words from Jesus. However,
the only way you can enjoy this peace is by keeping your
attention on God and His Word.

If you continue to focus on all the bad things happening in
the world, Satan will come to you with fearful thoughts,
trying to make you forget God's promises to protect and
keep you. I encourage you to keep a memory bank of the
things God has done for you. Thank Him, not only for what
He has done for you but also for what He has helped you
escape. Think of the times He has helped you. Think about
things you have received that you did not deserve. Just keep
remembering. Satan is trying to get your attention. Don't
let him have it; if you do, he will steal your peace.

When you watch the news and all the things going on that are hurting and taking the lives of people, the first thing you need to do is talk to Jesus. "Lord, you are my shepherd, and you told me you would give me peace. I am your child, and I am not afraid." Speak words of life rather than words of fear.

The only lasting way to keep Satan from stealing your peace is to know Jesus personally. He loves you and is reaching out. The problems won't go away, but you will never again be alone. Learn more about this in Chapter 10.

THINK AND SPEAK POSITIVELY ABOUT LIFE

Fear of the future grips the minds of people today as food, fuel, and other necessities of life grow out of control with their ever-rising costs. You cannot change what is, but you can set forth the course of your thinking and the words that come forth from your mouth. Instead of giving life to the negative and fearful things by speaking about them, begin to proclaim His Word and His promises. Think and speak about the *good things* that will inspire your faith instead of opening the door to fear.

Fear will hinder your faith and cause you to focus on the struggles and speak the negative things into this world, making them a reality. We live in days of much violence, evil, betrayal, selfishness, and a myriad of other negative influences. In the midst of the bad, ugly, and evil, there is a loving God who is ever-present to take your hand and lead you into safety.

And God will generously provide all you need. Then you will always have everything you need and plenty left over to share with others.
2 CORINTHIANS 9:8 NLT

Think, speak, and *act positively* about your life. Keep your conversations centered on God's abundant provision. Don't let words of lack and death fall from your lips. Speak living words.

> *Death and life are in the power of the tongue,*
> *And those who love it will eat its fruit.*
> PROVERBS 18:21

Satan will take every opportunity to introduce fear into any circumstance. Give *no place* to this wily one through your actions or your words.

Some teach that fear is the opposite of faith. This is true, but not the whole truth. *Love* is the opposite of *fear*. If you find yourself struggling with fearful thoughts and have been afraid, examine your love walk. When you become mature in your love walk with God, there is no room for fear.

> *There is no fear in love [dread does not exist]. But*
> *perfect (complete, full-grown) love drives out fear,*
> *because fear involves [the expectation of divine]*
> *punishment, so the one who is afraid [of God's*
> *judgment] is not perfected in love [has not grown*
> *into a sufficient understanding of God's love].*
> 1 JOHN 4:18 AMP

God's perfect love casts out all fear and every trace of terror. Love is greater than fear. Love believes the best, love is not fretful, love endures under pressure, love is not selfish and prideful, love is patient, and love rejoices when right and truth prevail. It is very important to walk in love if we want to live a life without fear.

WE CHOSE THE GOOD REPORT

When our daughter, Tammy, was in the hospital, we battled fearful thoughts, especially the first few days. She ran a high fever because of the head injuries and suffered seizures, one after the other. The doctors gave us no hope that she would even live through the night. The attending physicians would not set her broken bones, as they thought she would die before the sun came up—but she was a fighter and we were speaking life.

While we were wrestling with our fearful thoughts and feelings, we did our best to think on and speak God's promises and not allow what we were seeing to rob us of our peace. A friend came to see us at about 4:00 in the morning. He said, "Don't get your hopes up. Tammy is not going to make it. She is going to die." We had thought he was a man of faith. We anticipated words of encouragement from him, but he delivered fear and doubt.

We chose to encourage ourselves in the Lord. She did not die at the scene of the accident. We had hope and refused to focus on our friend's negative words. Our hope rested in God and not our friend's opinion or the dire circumstances before us. Sharon and I knew that love is greater than fear, and faith is stronger than any words to the contrary. Our faith stood firm on the Word of God, and we rebuked any and every fearful thought that stood contrary to His truth.

"No weapon formed against you shall prosper,
And every tongue which rises against you
in judgment You shall condemn. This is the
heritage of the servants of the LORD, And their
righteousness is from Me," Says the LORD.
ISAIAH 54:17

It was a long battle, especially on the eleventh morning after the accident. At 6:30 in the morning, the doctor came in and said, "There is no hope. Tammy is going to die. Prepare yourselves for the worst." But we knew that God—not the circumstances—was our source. I told the doctor I appreciated all he had done to help. He was a good Christian man. I informed him that my hope was in the Lord, not her present condition—and certainly not in the report he had just given me.

He said, "God is your only hope now. We have done all we can for her." At that moment, I began to think happy and good thoughts, sing a happy song, and speak life into our daughter, rather than allow the words of death to instill fear in my thoughts.

Moments after the doctor had given me the *bad report* that Tammy was going to die, a nurse came from the intensive care unit into the waiting room where I was stationed and gave me a *good report*. Immediately, I went into Tammy's room, and true enough, for the first time in eleven days we witnessed a positive change. She was only blinking her eyes, but that was enough for me. I phoned everyone I could to tell them Tammy was blinking her eyes! I ran throughout the hospital in those early hours of the morning and told everyone I saw, "Tammy is blinking her eyes!" I magnified the *good report* and put to rest the *bad report*. From that moment on, Tammy began to recover. Although she was still in critical condition, hope and progress began to unveil.

Tammy was released from the hospital about two months after the doctors informed us she was going to be a *vegetable* for the rest of her life—if she lived at all. We kept our faith in God, not in what we could see in the natural, and certainly not in the reports of her demise. Every day she improved until she was healed. God restored our daughter to life and health because we kept our minds on things that were *true* and things that were of *good report*, despite contrary evidence and bad reports.

Fear is dreadful and demoralizing. Too many live under this false life sentence and subjugate themselves to prophets of doom. Think yourself happy. Dismiss all notions and invitations that fear tries to deliver to your doorstep. You do not have to answer that door. Satan wants to deceive you and tries to force you to relinquish the most powerful weapon you have—*faith*—by chanting his songs of fear and defeat. Remember, when you allow Satan to deceive you and cause you to have fearful thoughts, you are believing the worst-case scenario, and fear grips you. Life is too short to live in the fear and terror of what *could happen*. Change your thinking, and *choose* to think on the things that will make you happy and free. Surround yourself with strong people of faith and positive people who love you. They will lift you up and support you. Keep your mind set on thinking happy thoughts, and enjoy life without fear.

ARE YOU STRUGGLING WITH FEAR?

Are you struggling with fear? What are you afraid of? Are you afraid of sickness, loneliness, or a shortage of funds in the midst of the economic turmoil? Perhaps you are afraid of what may happen to you as you age? Do you fear rejection or not being good enough to earn others' approval? Are you afraid of failure?

Intimidating thoughts of fear breed torment and enlarge the size of the problems you are facing. Fear does not come from God. Fear found its formation when the first man, Adam, sinned and was cast out of the Garden of Eden.

Before the fall of man, he was like God. He thought like God; he knew nothing of negative thoughts or ideas. He was made in the image and likeness of his Creator. He was not afraid of God because there was nothing to fear.

When Adam sinned, he lost his relationship with God and immediately became fearful, an emotion he and Eve had never before experienced. Before that happened, God visited him every day and talked with him. All that changed after he sinned.

God appeared in the garden and asked, "Adam, where are you?" He had never made such an inquiry before because Adam had always been waiting for God's visits with him. Adam answered, "I heard Your voice in the garden, and I was afraid because I was naked; and I hid myself" (Genesis 3:10). For the first time, Adam knew fear. He was naked and afraid, but the real issue was that he no longer had the covering of God's presence. He was confused and troubled in his thinking and had lost peace and direction for his life. He and Eve had allowed Satan to deceive them, and fear began.

Fear is deception. It is the *what-ifs* that form in your mind as you picture the worst scenarios that could happen to you. Fear exaggerates images in your mind and creates emotions of confusion, uncertainty, anxiety, worry, and more.

That fearful state of mind is the opposite of being happy. It is not possible to be happy when you are under the pressure of fear. How much of your life has been stolen and wasted because of fearful thoughts?

We must endeavor to exercise our rights as believers every day and think hopeful, encouraging, and peaceful thoughts. This kind of thinking opens the door for the Spirit of God within us as Christians and frees us from intimidating thoughts that plague us.

> *"You will keep in perfect and constant peace the one whose mind is steadfast [that is, committed and focused on You—in both inclination and character], Because he trusts and takes refuge in You [with hope and confident expectation]. Trust [confidently] in the LORD forever [He is your fortress, your shield, your banner], For the LORD GOD is an everlasting Rock [the Rock of Ages]."*
> ISAIAH 26:3–4 AMP

We have an enemy. His name is Satan. You can see from this passage of Scripture just how important it is to keep your mind and thoughts guarded against that enemy. The greatest battle is in your mind. One sure way to win this fight is by spending time daily in prayer and meditating on good things from God's Word. It's a spiritual battle. Leaving any door of your mind open to Satan gives him a foothold and the right to bombard you with fearful thoughts, making you afraid to face your tomorrows. He wants to keep you in fear of stepping out in faith and becoming the person God intended.

DON'T LET FEAR KEEP YOU FROM FULFILLING A DREAM!

Skydiving. I know it is not for everyone, but I often wondered what it would be like. I had contemplated trying it for more than ten years when my friend asked me to join him on a skydiving adventure. Only one minute of thought was required before a resounding yes fell from my lips.

We set a date. My son, who had decided to join me, and I rose early on the designated day to join my friend for the one-hour journey to the airfield. During this short drive, we discussed our thoughts and feelings about the adventure we were about to embark upon. My friend had made this jump once before, and he expounded with delight about his previous flight.

Arriving at the airport, we were presented with release forms we would have to sign. They stated we would not sue the company in the event of a tragedy. I didn't really believe anything would go wrong—but I admit that possibility had briefly crossed my mind.

Rather than focus on the danger, I made a conscious choice to not entertain negative thoughts. I am a child of God, and He has His angels watching over me!

After completing the paperwork, we received classroom instructions on what to expect, what to be prepared for, and how we were to position ourselves as we jumped. We were then required to show the instructor that we understood his directives by demonstrating on a floor mat what we had learned.

Suddenly, a touch of anxiety and nervousness attempted to mount up. *Where are these negative feelings coming from?* I wondered. I restrained myself from allowing such thoughts to dance around in my mind.

After finishing the preliminaries, we suited up in our jumpsuits and parachutes. I was very excited about what I was about to experience. I had looked forward to this for a long time, and now the dream of flying through the air was about to take place. We went outside by the grass-strip runway to wait our turn to climb aboard the airplane.

By this time, I was having a very positive adrenaline rush. As we sat waiting, suddenly the weather changed. We were notified that the winds had increased and it would not be possible to skydive that day. To say the least, it was a disappointment after we had done so much preparation—but in another way, a relief. We were told we would have to come another time, so we booked a new day to make the jump. Driving home, we talked excitedly about that upcoming date.

The day arrived. Sharon had decided to join us this second time out to observe our son David and me completing one of our dreams. Anticipation and excitement ruled the day. During the drive, we enthusiastically talked about the upcoming event. We all laughed and enjoyed our pre-jump discussions.

I began to praise God for the day and thank Him for His goodness. Philippians 4:8 echoed in my mind as I worshipped God and embraced His peace.

> *Finally, brethren, whatever things are true,*
> *whatever things are noble, whatever*
> *things are just, whatever things are pure, whatever*
> *things are lovely, whatever things are of good*
> *report, if there is any virtue and if there is anything*
> *praiseworthy—meditate on these things.*

I could have entertained the negativity of the previous attempt, but skydiving was something I truly wanted to experience. Fear and negative thoughts would not have a place in my life this time.

In an hour we arrived once again at the airfield and went through the same process of signing the consent forms and demonstrating to our instructor we had learned the proper procedures for the jump. The weather was perfect, all preflight procedures were complete, and now we were ready to ride our awaiting chariot into the sky.

The moment was filled with excitement, and adrenaline rushed through our beings. However, once again, fear attempted to grab me. The thought of blood pressure issues tried to darken my horizon.

During the brief walk toward the craft, more anxiety began to well up. I knew if I was to enjoy the experience, this foe could not be my partner. I was not about to miss out on this long-sought-after thrill of jumping and flying through the air.

Attempting to divert any thoughts that were trying to steal my joy, I began talking to the others who were about to share this experience with me. I climbed the ladder, stepped into the plane, and buckled myself in. The engine roared, the plane taxied down the runway, and we were off.

Along with being a pilot for many years, I had millions of miles of air travel under my belt, but this flight would be vastly different. I was not going to be landing in this plane; I would leave her mid-air and continue with a parachute.

Several experienced divers eagerly awaiting the thrill of yet another jump were sitting on the floor in front of us. The exhilarating thought of what lay ahead permeated their minds. As we discussed what was about to happen, suddenly I heard the engines slow down to our cruising speed for the leap as the plane leveled off. It was time for the big event of plunging into the air. I watched my companions jump one by one into infinity—or at least it seemed that way.

At this point, I scooted across the floor toward the open door. It was my turn. Anxiety greeted me as I inched toward the big open door, but I was determined to do what I had set out to accomplish. Oh boy, here I go! In a moment, I was free-falling at 120 miles per hour. An indescribable rush overwhelmed me. The sixty-second free fall was seven thousand feet, and then it was time to open the parachute. As my chute opened, there was a sudden unpleasant jerk— but that was such a good feeling.

Now the ride became quite different. I was in control of my direction, and a peaceful excitement flooded my soul. Soon I made a safe landing on my feet, exactly where I was supposed to land. Not one problem had transpired.

My skydiving adventure was memorable and exhilarating. I could have allowed my negative thoughts to keep me from making the dive, thus missing out on a truly wonderful and happy moment in my life. Instead, I chose to stick with it and will be forever thankful I overcame the fear.

IS FEAR HOLDING YOU BACK?

Is fear keeping you from fulfilling a dream? Perhaps a physical adventure like skydiving? Or entering a marathon? Or venturing into some other unknown territory? What things could you accomplish if negative thinking takes a back seat, and you choose to act on the positive instead? Philippians 4:8 instructs us to cast away the negative and *think on the positive*.

I encourage you to get out of your comfort zone and do something you have always wanted to do. Maybe God has called you to some kind of ministry. Have you let fear or negative thinking keep you from being everything God has called you to be? I was just fifteen years old when God called me into the ministry, and while I had no experience at that age, I knew God wanted me to go to many countries and preach the gospel. Even though I came from a large family that didn't have a lot, I chose to believe God that anything was possible if I put my trust in Him. I didn't know how all this would happen, but I did not let *where* I was become *who* I was.

My revelation was greater than my environment. I took one step at a time with my faith in God, and He opened doors I could never have opened. God gave me favor because I focused on His promises rather than on where I was at the moment. Now I rejoice in the Lord that He has taken me to places way beyond my dreams. Once again, I encourage you to let Jesus be the Lord of your life and think yourself happy every day in order to experience all He has in store for you. Don't let fear hold you back from fulfilling your dreams!

WHERE IS YOUR FOCUS?

Who or what has your attention? I speak and write this statement often: *Don't allow yourself to be emotionally ruled.* This is where Satan gets his greatest success with Christians. When you give in to your feelings and emotions, your thinking becomes negative, and you lose your peace and give way to fear.

Sure, we are aware of what is happening around us, and sometimes to us, but we must not give all our attention to that. Instead, we should set our minds on who God is and His promises to us.

Don't allow fear to be your master.

Chapter 3

Worry

Worry and *fear* are intertwined. Worry is meditating or continually thinking on the things that may never happen, things over which you have no control. Worry is the dark room where negatives are developed. If you think on the wrong things, then worry will cause you to lose your peace, and fear will grip you. Worrying is a waste of time. It accomplishes nothing positive and creates havoc with your emotions. A pattern of worry can even cause physical illness.

Nothing is sadder to God and mankind than a wasted life. How many times have you heard about the untimely death of a talented performer or the moral downfall of a brilliant public servant and said to yourself, "What a sad waste of talent and potential"? But waste is not achieved in one fell swoop; waste is achieved one baby step at a time. And I don't believe anything wastes more of our precious time in tiny pieces than worry. Worry is probably the worst investment of our time and energy that we can make.

Wasted Thoughts = Wasted Moments

Wasted Moments = Wasted Hours

Wasted Hours = Wasted Days

Wasted Days = Wasted Weeks

Wasted Weeks = Wasted Months

Wasted Months = Wasted Years

Wasted Years = Wasted LIFE

Mark Twain once said, "I've had a lot of worries in my life, most of which never happened."[1] Like most of us, he invested days and hours of his precious free time—time that could have been spent writing more books—on things that weren't even real and on things that never came to pass. He threw away all that irreplaceable time—the most precious gift God had entrusted to him—on something that had no substance.

How much of your irretrievable time have you wasted worrying about things that never happened? Have you wasted moments—or even years—on fruitless endeavors? How much of your mental and emotional energy have you squandered on problems that eventually resolved themselves? Is it possible you have lost out on opportunities in life because you allowed unproductive thoughts to control your mind? The *what-if* and *if-only* thoughts? Is it possible you have missed open doors that God set before you because you were preoccupied with thinking based on imaginations and *what-ifs* rather than on reality? What a sad, sad thought! But the fact is that all of us have wasted our time and potential by allowing our minds to take us down rabbit trails of worry.

Worrying about problems over which we have no control diminishes what should be the lion's share of our thought life and confidence in Jesus. Opportunities are lost, time becomes unproductive, and ultimately, the fruit of our lives

---

1   Twain, Mark. Quoted in "Mark Twain>Quotes>Quotable Quote," Goodreads: https://www.goodreads.com/quotes/201777-i-ve-had-a-lot-of-worries-in-my-life-most.

is severely crippled by *wasted thoughts*. It is my prayer that as you read this chapter, you will choose to surrender worry and instead trust fully in the Lord.

FAITH VERSUS WORRY

A faith-filled Christian couple embarked on a two-week cruise to get away from the busyness of their lives. Looking forward to this adventure together, they dreamed of new sights and experiences of grandeur that would be unveiled to them on the open sea. But the unexpected soon shipwrecked those plans.

Arriving at the point of the cruise ship's launch, they were greeted by the ship's crew. Suitcases were checked in and their small carry-on bags were toted. They were comforted by the confident words of the crew that all personal belongings would await them in their private cabin. As they made their way there, they found the larger luggage containing clothes and toiletries, but no sign of the smaller personal bags carrying medicines and valuables was to be found. They asked the crew about the whereabouts of the smaller carry-on bags. Assurances of the pending arrival of the missing bags brought comfort, and they began their exploration of all the beautiful cruise ship had to offer.

The couple discovered that vast varieties of unending food were available. The opulence of the vessel offered many photo opportunities. A seemingly unending schedule of things to do convinced them they had made a grand decision. After several hours of inventorying all the cruise ship had to offer, they decided to return to their cabin. At a glance, it was obvious their smaller bags were not there. Hours passed and night began to fall, but the missing-in-action bags had still not arrived.

Not knowing what else they could humanly do, the couple began to pray, asking the Lord to locate and return to them the missing luggage. The wife beseeched the Lord, saying, "This situation is in your hands, and I trust you that all lost would soon be found and returned." She practiced casting all her cares on the Lord, as instructed in 1 Peter 5:7: "Give all your worries and cares to God, for he cares about you" (NLT). Filled with peace in knowing all was in God's hands, she was ready to continue enjoying their long-planned vacation. On the other end of the spectrum, her husband decided that *worry* was the appropriate action to take, even though his wife encouraged him that this situation was in God's hands.

The following morning, the missing bags had still not arrived. The ship's doctor was sought, as they needed replacements for their medicines. She remained in peace; he remained in turmoil. Her thoughts rested in faith, knowing and trusting in the everlasting God. He remained true to the previous day's worry that someone had stolen the valuables. His continued vain search only bolstered his negative thoughts and attitude.

The man's emotions and anger spurred on more worry, which prevailed over his thought life. Rather than enjoying the utopia of these two weeks in paradise, he could entertain only worry as his friend. His wife's continued faith-filled encouragement fell on deaf ears. She was at peace, while misery was his closest companion. He let worry reign. Money and time were wasted in the throes of lamenting what *should have been*. When the cruise was coming to an end, they learned the missing bags had finally been found.

The cruise they had so eagerly anticipated was now over. And while the wife had thoroughly enjoyed herself, her husband had fretted the whole time. He too could have had a great time with a simple change of attitude—but he chose to worry. The wasted thoughts that preoccupied his mind became poisonous seeds that sapped all the joy from his cruise.

They both had faced the same situation. Although the wife was genuinely concerned about her valuables, she made a conscious decision to enjoy her vacation rather than fret over circumstances she could not control. She made a deliberate choice to trust God. Of course, she wanted her luggage back, but she could not control the situation, so she decided not to worry.

But her husband was obsessed with the problem. He worried constantly about his misplaced luggage and the possible loss of his valuables, so he allowed his negative expectations of the outcome, not the outcome itself, to torture him and ruin his entire vacation. They had paid a lot of money for this cruise, a cruise he chose not to enjoy.

Jesus said, "Let not your heart be troubled; you believe in God, believe also in Me" (John 14:1). If you worry, you will have bad feelings. And the worse you feel, the worse things will get for you. Choose instead to bless yourself with happy thoughts. Thoughts of trusting God and leaving things in His hands.

More encouraging words from Jesus:

> *"That is why I tell you not to worry about everyday life—whether you have enough food and drink, or enough clothes to wear. Isn't life more than food, and your body more than clothing? Look at the birds. They don't plant or harvest or store food in barns, for your heavenly*

Father feeds them. And aren't you far more valuable to him than they are? Can all your worries add a single moment to your life?

"And why worry about your clothing? Look at the lilies of the field and how they grow. They don't work or make their clothing, yet Solomon in all his glory was not dressed as beautifully as they are. And if God cares so wonderfully for wildflowers that are here today and thrown into the fire tomorrow, he will certainly care for you. Why do you have so little faith?

"So don't worry about these things, saying, 'What will we eat? What will we drink? What will we wear?' These things dominate the thoughts of unbelievers, but your heavenly Father already knows all your needs. Seek the Kingdom of God above all else, and live righteously, and he will give you everything you need."
MATTHEW 6:25–33 NLT

The Lord has instructed us not to worry about our life, our future, what we eat, or what we wear. Your future is in His hands. Give it to Him. Instead of trying to be in control of everything, allow Him to help you. The Word says, "We can make our own plans, but the LORD gives the right answer" (Proverbs 16:1 NLT).

If you place your life in God's hands, He will help you. *Worry* will not add one inch to your stature. Worrying over things will never produce good fruit in your life. What it will produce is fear, depression, and long, unhappy days and nights. Life is too short to live worrying over things you cannot change or things that may not ever happen.

SET YOUR THOUGHTS TO BE PRODUCTIVE

What has your mind been set on as you read this book? What have your thoughts been set on for the past few days?

I have two thermostats in my home. I set them to whatever temperature I want in my house, and the unit goes to work to achieve and maintain the desired temperature. It's the same thing with our thoughts; we must set them on things that will bring the results we want.

If you constantly change the thermostat setting, you will never get the temperature you want. If you keep changing your mind and never settle on right thoughts, you will never find peace and happiness.

If you think about food all the time, that's what your mind is set on, and what you think on the most is what you will do. A few nights ago after our dinner, I kept thinking about ice cream. The next thing I knew, I went to the freezer and began dipping a couple of scoops of ice cream into my dish. There is nothing wrong with a little bit of ice cream, but if I thought about it all the time and ate it every day, that would not be a good thing for my body.

Likewise, it's not healthy for you to set your mind on *what-ifs*. It's not healthy to focus on worry.

Begin by setting your thoughts on God's Word. Focus on His love and promises rather than on worry about what may happen. Settle His Word in your thoughts and heart. Believe that He loves you. Only He knows what is best for you, and only He can truly provide what you need. Learn to rest in Him.

PEACE IS THE GLUE

I believe peace is the glue of a successful Christian life. It's one of our most valuable assets. If this is not true, then why is the enemy always trying to steal it from us? A lack of peace affects our whole being— spiritually, emotionally, physically, financially, and relationally.

Worry closes our minds to truth, to God's voice. But the peace that comes by setting our minds on Him keeps our minds open to hear from God and helps us make good decisions and enjoy life.

When you are not at peace and trusting God when something unexpected comes, it keeps you from sleep and enjoying your life. It disrupts everything. If you do not want to slide into fear and confusion, go back to where you lost your peace and do whatever it is you need to get it back. Peace will help guide you and allow you to hear God's voice.

> *And let the peace of God rule in your*
> *hearts, to which also you were called*
> *in one body; and be thankful.*
> COLOSSIANS 3:15

One of the keys to a successful life is learning how to walk in peace. Fear and worry are unproductive and disabling. Are you allowing someone or something to rob you of your peace daily? Ask God what steps you need to take to find peace again.

PRAY

You may say, "I do not want to worry, but I still find myself fretting about things I have no control over." Worry is thinking about the things you don't want to happen. It takes time to overcome negative thoughts of worry. This is not going to be an overnight fix, but you have to start somewhere, and I encourage you to start now.

You will need to take authority over your thoughts. Speak something like this: "In Jesus' name, I will no longer worry. I choose to focus on Jesus and to trust Him. I choose to think positive thoughts based on His name and His love." Ask God to help deliver you from all negative thoughts. Praying and spending time praising God will set the stage for your freedom.

> *We use God's mighty weapons, not worldly*
> *weapons, to knock down the strongholds of*
> *human reasoning and to destroy false arguments.*
> 2 CORINTHIANS 10:4 NLT

If negative thoughts and imaginations are affecting your life, let me help you. Negative thinking is taking you nowhere and is keeping you from happiness and enjoying your life. You can't "fix" this on your own—you need to trust God for His peace. Here are three things to start your victorious turnaround from negative thinking and worrying.

1. Find a private place to pray without distractions. Tell God you really want to change your life, to stop worrying and instead trust Him. Ask Him to free you from worry, from negative and doubt-filled thoughts. Jesus said this:

   > *"Therefore do not worry or be anxious*
   > *(perpetually uneasy, distracted), saying,*
   > *'What are we going to eat?' Bor 'What are*
   > *we going to drink?' or 'What are we going*
   > *to wear?' For the [pagan] Gentiles eagerly*
   > *seek all these things; [but do not worry,] for*

*your heavenly Father knows that you need
them. But first and most importantly seek
(aim at, strive after) His kingdom and His
righteousness [His way of doing and being
right—the attitude and character of God], and
all these things will be given to you also."*
MATTHEW 6:31–33 AMP

2. Find people of faith who are spiritual and positive. Spend time with them, pray with them, and let them know you want to change. Be accountable to them. You may not want them to know the kind of negative thoughts you have battled, but realize that everyone has to deal with them at times. Make sure you have people in your life who care about you and your future.

*Therefore encourage and comfort one
another and build up one another.*
1 THESSALONIANS 5:11 AMP

3. Find a good church that teaches His Word. Attend regularly. Get involved and serve other people. As you minister to others, you will find yourself thinking less about yourself. Spend time in prayer, and worship the Lord. Nothing is greater than being in God's presence.

*Trust in and rely confidently on the LORD with
all your heart And do not rely on your own
insight or understanding. In all your ways
know and acknowledge and recognize Him, And
He will make your paths straight and smooth
[removing obstacles that block your way].*
PROVERBS 3:5–6 AMP

While praying, I spend time praying for others, and I take time to give God praise for my life and His blessings. I thank Him for all the opportunities I have had to bless many around the world. As I pray, His presence and joy flood my soul. As I do all these things, God gives me peace over things I cannot change or control. You can find this same kind of peace.

I hope you will begin to take these steps today. Give up those things you can't control. Choose God's plan—and His peace.

Chapter 4

Self-Doubt

Do you like yourself? Do you begin each day with confidence?

Or . . . have you allowed other people's opinions to shape the way you see yourself? Have you allowed other people's plans for your life to dictate your choices and even your beliefs? Have you heard their put-downs so often and for so long that you believe them yourself? Or are you letting past failures paint your opinion of yourself? Do you think about such things as if they were true?

The way you think about yourself forms the way you behave. "For as he thinks in his heart, so is he" (Proverbs 23:7).

BEN: THINKING TRANSFORMED

I once read a story about a man from Tennessee named Ben Hopper. He was labeled as an illegitimate child, living in a time when it was difficult for anyone with this label to be accepted by society. Ben lived with constant criticism. He was ridiculed because he did not know who his father was. It seemed as though all odds were stacked against him.

Ben had not chosen his circumstances, but those circumstances shaped the way he thought about himself.

Time took its toll on this young man. Because of the criticism, he became extremely shy and insecure.

Ben loved to go to church but was reluctant because of the ugly things people would say to him. Then a new minister came to town. The people of the area embraced him, and he quickly won their hearts. Ben decided to attend a service and check out this new pastor. Sitting in the back corner of the church by himself, he hoped he could avoid others and any negative comments they may hurl his way.

The service was good, and the joy of the minister's message caused Ben to stay longer than he had anticipated. Since he had missed his opportunity to escape unnoticed, anxiety began to creep its way into his mind. Doing his best to flee the premises undetected, he found himself face-to-face with the new minister. Not knowing what to do or say, he chose to simply be quiet.

Then the new preacher said to him, "Whose boy are you?"

This was exactly the scenario Ben had hoped to avoid. His mind flooded with the thought, *Even the preacher is going to judge me because I don't have a father.*

The minister saw the fear in Ben's countenance. Peering into the young man's eyes, he said kindly, "I know who you are, son. I can see the family resemblance—you are a child of God."

As they parted ways, the minister patted Ben on the back. "You have a great inheritance; now go and claim it!"

Those precious words spoke life to Ben's soul. Even though he was a poor boy who did not know who his father was . . . even though society's odds were stacked against him . . . these words from a man of God caused Ben to see himself in an all new way. Hope filled his mind; dreams filled his heart. Because of this new, radical thinking, change came to young Ben. He was no longer chained to his circumstances or to the opinions of others. Years later, in 1911, he became the governor of Tennessee and served two terms.

HOW ABOUT YOU?

Have you allowed people's opinions and critical tongues to shape the person you see in the mirror? Have you allowed the negative voices of others to become your reality?

Or perhaps you have convinced yourself, maybe because of past failures, that you will never succeed. That you are a "loser."

Has that kind of thinking become your reality?

That's not how God sees you.

Stop listening and looking through the lens of what other people are telling you. Look beyond them. Stop seeing yourself as a loser. You are a child of God, and you can do anything God created you to do. You can be anything God has planned for you to be.

You are special to God. He knew you before you were born, and He loves you unconditionally. He loves you so much, He sent His only Son, Jesus, to die for your sins. Every sin was nailed to that cross; every work of darkness was rendered powerless. Jesus came and conquered Satan so you might have a rich and abundant life. If you don't have a personal relationship with Him, take a moment now to learn how you can take that step in chapter 10.

The thief cometh not, but for to steal, and to kill,
and to destroy: I am come that they might have

life, and that they might have it more abundantly.
JOHN 10:10 KJV

No matter what your life has been like in the past, the Lord can take you where He is calling you if you will trust His Word. Your circumstances do not have the authority to keep you in bondage. Refuse to offer up excuses as to why you cannot be happy. Relinquish every opportunity to settle for less than His best because of the battles that rage inside you.

You cannot change the past, but you can change the way you think from this point forward. Allowing feelings of unworthiness while striving for happiness is a contradiction. Do not buy the lie. His Word alone stands as truth. Has a family member ever told you, "You will never be anybody, never amount to anything"? If so, then realize this death sentence over your future does not have to be your reality. What the Lord says about you can be established as your reality for all your tomorrows.

If you find your mind going to a dark place, dwelling on a disadvantage you may perceive to be real, you do not have to set up permanent camp in this province. You are not an accident. Your obstacles may be real, but God can help you think about the possibilities instead of the hindrances at hand. As a child of God, trust that He is leading you into something good. What He proclaims about you should be more real to you than any emotional or physical limitations others may try to pronounce over you.

For I know the thoughts that I think toward
you, says the LORD, thoughts of peace and
not of evil, to give you a future and a hope.
JEREMIAH 29:11

GIDEON FELT UNWORTHY

In the book of Judges, we see the story of Gideon unfold. Gideon was called to a God-ordained mission, but he felt unworthy of the purpose to which he was called. God commissioned him to bring deliverance and freedom to Israel in a very dark hour.

And the Angel of the LORD appeared to him, and said to him, "The LORD is with you, you mighty man of valor!"

Gideon said to Him, "O my lord, if the LORD is with us, why then has all this happened to us? And where are all His miracles which our fathers told us about, saying, 'Did not the LORD bring us up from Egypt?' But now the LORD has forsaken us and delivered us into the hands of the Midianites."

Then the LORD turned to him and said, "Go in this might of yours, and you shall save Israel from the hand of the Midianites. Have I not sent you?"

So he said to Him, "O my Lord, how can I save Israel? Indeed my clan is the weakest in Manasseh, and I am the least in my father's house."

And the LORD said to him, "Surely I will be with you, and you shall defeat the Midianites as one man."
JUDGES 6:12–16

Gideon weighed in on this assignment with little confidence. He said his family was the weakest in his tribe, and he was the least in his family. Even though Gideon's perception of himself did not rise to that challenge and purpose, the Lord called him a "mighty man of valor." The angel encouraged him to go forth in God's might and power. The Lord proclaimed He would be with Gideon, and Gideon would defeat the Midianites as if he were fighting against one man.

Gideon decided to reject the toxic thoughts of timidity and man's interpretation and perception about who he was. He decided to believe what God had said and trust in God's power. Taking three hundred men, he descended into the enemy's camp of thousands and won the battle. Never could he have dreamed the Lord would use him in such a magnificent measure, but He did. Gideon lived the words of the prophet Zechariah: "'Not by might nor by power, but by My Spirit,' Says the Lord of hosts" (Zechariah 4:6).

The Lord ultimately raised up Gideon to release the children of Israel in great victory. Although Gideon's initial reaction to this call had been laden with doubt, the angel did not see him in his present situation—he saw this young man as what he would soon become.

This is exactly how God sees you. He sees your potential. He sees what He has called you to do. Others may not recognize your bestowed capability, but that does not matter. What the Lord sees stands as absolute truth.

You may say, "Well, that was Gideon, and it is different because this is a person from the Bible." God has given you this biblical example for a reason!

Isaiah 54:17 says, "No weapon that is formed against you shall prosper." A parent, spouse, or teacher may have spoken negative things about you, but their words do not make those things true. You see your limitations, but God sees none. All things are possible for those who believe. "I can do all things through Christ who strengthens me" (Philippians 4:13).

You are an overcomer. You are God's champion. Like Gideon, you may not believe you can accomplish great things, but you have the potential to do anything you believe you can do. Believe you can accomplish what God has placed inside your heart.

Your history is a record of your past; your potential is a promise for your future. Be careful about writing your future story prematurely because of your past. Other people may judge you according to your history, and you may tend to judge yourself by the same standard. God specializes in forgiving the past and focusing on the future. You must do the same as you learn from your history and draw from it while focusing on your future potential.

Andrew Carnegie became wealthy when he stopped seeing himself as a poor lad from Scotland, only to almost single-handedly build the American steel industry. Gideon became a mighty warrior when he stopped thinking of himself in lowly terms, only to be used by God to defeat an army of three hundred thousand with just three hundred men.

Change your thinking. Believe what God is telling you about yourself in His Word and in your heart.

> *For You formed my inward parts; You covered me*
> *in my mother's womb. I will praise You, for I am*
> *fearfully and wonderfully made; Marvelous are*
> *Your works, And that my soul knows very well.*
> PSALM 139:13–14

RIGHT THINKING OPENS DOORS

I come from a wonderfully large family. There were eight children, and we did not have much in the realm of material things. I was the seventh child, shy and insecure. I did not have a dream. I was void of goals until I became a Christian and was called into the ministry.

When I was only fifteen, God called me into the ministry to preach the gospel, and a fire began to burn inside me to help people around the world. I didn't know how to make this dream a reality, but I immersed myself in the Word of God and every Christian book about living by faith I could get my hands on. As I studied His Word, I believed more in what God had called me to do than in my weaknesses I was aware of. I thought, "If God can believe in me, then surely I can believe in myself." Dreams to help people around the world began to grow inside me.

My desire to help people was inspired by Matthew 14:14, where Jesus saw the multitude, was moved with compassion for them, and healed the sick. I was overcome with this vision. I knew that somehow it would be possible, even though I was young and still in school. I did not know how to get from where I was to the place God was calling me. All I knew was that God had put this great desire in me to communicate the compassion of Jesus and demonstrate the healing power of His Word. I knew I could not do any of this on my own. I would have to have His help. I focused on Him. I made it my purpose in life to seek His will and His way—and change my thinking.

I found myself immersed in His Word, at times staying up all night seeking His face. I felt like Gideon. In myself, I did not believe I possessed what it would take to fulfill this call, but I knew if I would follow His direction, He would help me. My mother was my greatest source of comfort. She stormed the gates of heaven fervently on my behalf, praying I would successfully reach the people the Lord had assigned to my life.

I could have given in to my insecurities. The shyness and weakness could have ruled my life. However, I chose to press through these things, think good thoughts, and surround myself with people who believed in me and the dream God had given me. Memorizing Scripture became a priority. Attending services at the church was the norm; every time the doors opened, I would be there. Serving the Lord and others was my focus and purpose in life.

The Word says, "Who [with reason] despises the day of small things (beginnings)?" (Zechariah 4:10 AMP). Don't be afraid to start small!

Soon, I watched God open doors in countries where I had never been and where no one knew my name, yet thousands would come and miracles would flood the fields filled with people. Presidents and people of great influence sought my counsel and prayer. The road has not always been easy, but my faith has always rested in the God who called me.

HAKUNA MATATA: DON'T WORRY, BE HAPPY

Disney's *The Lion King* is a great example of how people can get off on the wrong track. The young lion, Simba, was in line to become the next king; however, his Uncle Scar was filled with jealousy. Scar desired to be king, so he blamed Simba for the death of Simba's father, Mufasa. It was not Simba's fault that Mufasa was dead, but Scar lied and placed that guilt on the young lion.

Although Simba was not guilty, he accepted the blame and took on all the guilt, forcing him to run away from the family that loved him. He turned a deaf ear to the responsibility of being heir to the throne. His self-image was marred, and confidence in his future was destroyed because of wrong thinking. He allowed his thoughts to convince him he was worthless. Pumbaa and Timon, a warthog and a meerkat, convinced him to live in a fantasy world and escape the real issues he should have faced.

They adopted a catchphrase that expressed their philosophy of life: "Hakuna Matata," which means "no worries." With their encouragement, Simba ignored the things he should have taken responsibility for and created his own false sense of reality. Then he came face to face with his lioness friend, Nala, who challenged him to get his thoughts realigned. Nala knew he was destined to become king.

Simba began to listen to Nala. Her encouragement caused him to reevaluate his thoughts. Simba had grown up physically but did not realize his growth or the size to which he had matured. In his own eyes, Simba was still the little lion cub. In his mind, he was still small and insignificant. Insecurity reigned over his life. Even though he was strong on the outside, inner conflict and debate in his mind brought about confusion and worry.

One day, Rafiki, a former friend of Mufasa, led Simba to a quiet pool of water, where he gazed upon his reflection; he looked like King Mufasa. Seeing himself as he was instead of the image his guilt-ridden, worried thoughts had produced, he returned home to face his enemies and take back the pride and the land. Soon Simba learned Scar had been responsible for the death of his father.

Scar had infiltrated Simba's mind with lies, and the deception had become real. Rejecting the old thinking and rising to be who he was born to be, Simba took his rightful place as king.

I know this is a cute animated Disney story about a lion cub, but there is a great lesson here. What you think becomes your reality, even if the things you think are simply not true. You will always act on your most dominant thoughts. If you think you are defeated, defeat will prevail. The things we think about can limit our relationships, opportunities, and successes in life. Embracing negative thinking and acting on negative thoughts will ensure a life of defeat.

Although *The Lion King* is a made-up story, it is impactful because it is founded upon reality. It is based upon a universal experience that has deprived far too many people of their destiny and significance. That is why so many people, including adults, identify with the characters and the plot of this film.

Far too many people believe false things about themselves. Far too many people embrace incorrect appraisals of their own worth. Far too many people abandon their hopes, dreams, and goals because they see themselves as incapable or unworthy of those ideals. Far too many people escape into a make-believe world where they can hide among new friends who can help them avoid dealing with the real issues of their lives. And far too many people sit on the sidelines, allowing the enemy to destroy their own lives and the lives of others because they choose to listen to the voices of guilt and condemnation that wrongly accuse them of things they have not done or things that should not be allowed to destroy their future potential.

The lesson of this story is that what you think becomes your reality, even if it is untrue. You act upon the most dominant thoughts of your mind. You must recognize negative and deceptive thoughts, appreciate their power to control the course of your life, and then do something positive to change them.

Your thoughts control you—they really do. If you think you are defeated, then you are. If you think you will never achieve anything in life, then you won't. If you think you might fail, then you will. Far too many people have limited their relationships, their opportunities, and their achievements by choosing to believe false or limiting things about themselves. They have embraced a lie and, like Simba, have allowed their unfounded beliefs to create a new reality.

Fortunately, God has provided us with a reflecting pool. He has provided us with a *mirror*, which, like the pool of water in *The Lion King*, is designed to give us a clear and accurate picture of who we are. The mirror that always accurately reflects the truth is the mirror of God's Word.

> *For if you listen to the word and don't obey,*
> *it is like glancing at your face in a mirror. You*
> *see yourself, walk away, and forget what*
> *you look like. But if you look carefully into*
> *the perfect law that sets you free, and if you*
> *do what it says and don't forget what you*
> *heard, then God will bless you for doing it.*
> JAMES 1:23–25 NLT

So, God has given us a mechanism through which we can see ourselves completely and accurately. The Word of God is our mirror. It is our measuring rod for the truth about ourselves. No longer should we rely on the opinions of others when we seek an accurate appraisal of ourselves. No longer should we rely on the twisted beliefs we often hold about ourselves. Instead, we should believe the things God has said about us in His written Word.

In the same way his reflection in the pool of water awakened Simba to the truth and inspired him to take action to change his situation, the mirror of God's Word must prompt us to take action if it is to be helpful in our lives. James explains that nothing is more foolish than to stare into a mirror, noticing imperfections about oneself, and then walk away as if those imperfections weren't even there. The purpose of a mirror is to reveal to us the disheveled hair, the little dab of toothpaste on the cheek, or the tiny cold sore on the upper lip so we can do something about those imperfections before other people notice them too. A mirror gives us the information we need so we can act upon it. Simba acted upon the information he discovered while staring into his "mirror." What do you intend to do to act upon the information God shares with you regarding your value and your worth?

God's Word instructs us to be *doers* of His Word and not *hearers* only. This is the beginning of change. We must listen to God's directions (thinking is a vital part of listening) and then incorporate them into our daily lives. Change comes by taking steps of obedience. Happiness is a choice every person can make regardless of circumstances. However, we are required to push through the things we are facing.

The Bible tells us to go to the mirror of His Word and look to see God's image in us. Scripture reminds us who we are and what we truly look like. Other people's opinions and accusations will not determine who we are if we allow what He has said to become our reality. "For as he thinks in his heart, so is he" (Proverbs 23:7).

How do you see yourself? Do your thoughts hold you back? Does your thinking limit you? Have bad seeds planted by others through criticism limited your ability to achieve? Have you been afraid to get out of your comfort zone because of what others have said about you? God wants you to be happy, and He has made provision for you to overcome every negative thing that has, or will, come against you.

What has God called you to become?

YOU ARE RIGHTEOUS

Have you received Jesus as your personal Savior? If so, you have been born again. If not, learn more about how you can take this step in Chapter 10.

> *Jesus replied, "I assure you, no one can enter*
> *the Kingdom of God without being born of*
> *water and the Spirit. Humans can reproduce*
> *only human life, but the Holy Spirit gives*
> *birth to spiritual life. So don't be surprised*
> *when I say, 'You must be born again.'"*
> JOHN 3:5–7 NLT

If you are born again, then it is time for you to understand who you are. You are the righteousness of God, in Christ. When you accepted Jesus as your Lord, God gave you His righteousness. What Christ did on the cross is your gift that no man can take from you—it is free. *It is yours!*

> *For He made Him who knew no sin to*
> *be sin for us, that we might become*
> *the righteousness of God in Him.*
> 2 CORINTHIANS 5:21

Although Jesus never sinned, on the cross He took the sin of this world upon Himself. He became sin for us. Even though we are not worthy of His righteousness, it is ours. After we receive Jesus as our Savior, God looks at us and sees us clothed in the righteousness of Christ.

> *I am overwhelmed with joy in the LORD my*
> *God! For he has dressed me with the clothing of*
> *salvation and draped me in a robe of righteousness.*
> ISAIAH 61:10 NLT

Righteousness means that you are now in right standing with God. Once you are cleansed of your sin, you are His child, and you walk in this new birth. Hold your head high. Be happy. Enjoy life. His righteousness brings you confidence.

Don't let criticism (aimed at you by others or by yourself) dominate your life. You may not be as educated as some. You may not have the arsenal of gifts they possess. You may not have the looks of those in your world, and your bank account balance may seem anemic compared with those around you. But as a born-again believer, be mindful of whose child you are. You are a child of the King of kings!

BE ENCOURAGED . . . AND ENCOURAGE OTHERS

Don't allow negative words in a situation to lead and control your life in the wrong direction. They will weigh you down. Instead, allow encouraging words from God's Word and from others to lift you up.

> *Anxiety in a man's heart weighs it down, But*
> *a good (encouraging) word makes it glad.*
> PROVERBS 12:25 AMP

I am an encourager. My entire life and ministry are about helping people become all God created them to be. My desire is that this book will help you become *all* God has intended *you* to be!

Satan is the enemy of your soul. He knows your potential *in Christ,* and he fears it. But he knows he can neutralize your God-given potential if he convinces you to think negatively about yourself. He will try to do that by constantly bombarding you with the negative words of others until you marinate in the lies and let them seep into the pores of your mind.

Negative people will constantly remind you that there is someone who has a better education, someone who has more money, someone who has more gifts and talents, someone who is healthier, stronger, better looking, and in better shape. But don't let their criticisms get to you. In the end, none of these things matter anyway. All that really matters is *who you are* and *whose you are.* And you belong to the Lord.

So be encouraged by the way God sees you and by all the uplifting things He has to say about you in His Word. Let the truth of what God says about you become the launching pad from which you begin to change your thinking so He can change your life.

Although the hurtful and critical words of others can inflict an immense amount of pain and give rise to a multitude of doubts, one word from God through a fellow believer, one word from God through a church service, one word from God through the Bible, or one word from God that flows from the faith that is deep within your own heart can put you on the road to happiness and a life that is glorious and well worth living.

A pastor commented that an elderly lady in his church was like a magnet because everybody was drawn to her. When he got to know her better, he was surprised at how difficult her life had been. She had nursed an invalid husband for ten years before he died, and her children said he'd been a cranky and demanding husband. Her married children had brought her a lot of heartache over the years, but she remained a cheerful and loving person with a great sense of humor. Finally, the pastor asked this lady what her secret was. She replied that it was simple. When she got up each morning, she had two choices: to be happy or to be unhappy. It was obvious which she chose. You have that same choice, no matter what you may be experiencing in your life at the moment. Choose to see yourself as God does—and think yourself happy.

HOW DO YOU LOOK AT YOURSELF?

In the end, there are three ways to look at yourself. You can look at yourself the way other people see you . . . you can look at yourself the way you currently see yourself . . . or you can look at yourself the way God sees you. We have already seen that other people may shortchange you in their appraisals. Quite often, even your parents and your siblings may doubt your character and your abilities. And you, like many others, may have an incorrect appraisal of yourself. You may think either too highly or too lowly of yourself. You may be driven by either a bloated ego or depressing self-loathing.

But God sees you just right. He sees you the way you are. And He sees all the potential He placed within you even before you were born. He sees you the way He created you to be, and He sees you the way you will be when He finishes all the reconstruction that is underway right now in your life.

So, the best way to see yourself is the way God sees you. The best way to think about yourself is the way God thinks about you. Right now, the Lord sees you the way you are going to be when He is finished doing all His work in your life. He is focusing on who you will be, not on the person you are today. He sees the *mighty warrior* within you. You need to do the same.

Even if you don't believe God can do this for you, God believes in you. He knows He has given you everything you need to make the journey from where you are to where He wants you to be. But you have to stop listening to the doubters and the false appraisers—even if those voices are coming from inside your head—and start listening to what God is saying about you. Yes, you have obstacles to navigate. Yes, you have wounds to treat. But every great man and every great woman have had challenges in life. Nevertheless, they overcame those challenges because of the strength of heart that God gave them—and you can do the same.

Chapter 5

Unforgiveness

Do you find it difficult to forgive others when they have hurt you? Offended you? Betrayed you? Perhaps even abused you?

Holding on to hurts of the past will make you miserable. Staying angry and refusing to forgive does not punish the offender—but that choice does hurt you. Holding on to offenses against you will keep the pain alive in you.

If you harbor unforgiveness and resentment, you may not be in a literal prison with bars on your cell, but you will live in the prison of *emotional bondage*. You will have a diminished quality of life instead of living the life Christ wants to give you.

Will you continue to allow yourself to be a hostage by constantly warring with yourself and entertaining unhappy thoughts? If you don't want to pay that price, you don't have to. Again, trusting Jesus to help you, you can change your thinking to line up with what we learn in the Bible about forgiveness.

BITTER . . . OR BETTER?

The painful things you experience in life can make you bitter or better. It's your choice.

If hurts have chained you to your past, the words penned in this book will help guide you to freedom. Choices you make today will determine your future. *Unforgiveness* will hinder God's blessings from flowing in your life, making happiness elusive.

Forgiveness is not a popular topic to address or an easy one to adopt into your life if you have been unfairly hurt or wronged by another. Proving to be the stronger person by forgiving is not easily accomplished when you have done no wrong. *Why should they be let off the hook when they were clearly in the wrong?* It is easy to want to get even rather than offering forgiveness to the offender. *Why should I be the one extending the gift of forgiveness when they have taken something from me? They should be apologizing to me.*

Let me spoon up this dollop, even though you may not find it palatable at first taste: Forgiveness is never about someone else. It is about *you*! Your first thought may be, *Preposterous!* No, it's true. Someone else may have treated you wrong, but forgiveness is for your benefit. Forgiveness can bring you peace. Ultimately, your freedom has nothing to do with the offender. Your decision to pardon them is an act of your will and separates you from the offense. Their act cannot be undone; therefore, you need to forgive and move forward.

Will you let their actions keep you bitter—or will you become better?

YOU CAN NEVER BE PAID BACK FOR YOUR LOSS

If you have been the victim of emotional or physical abuse, you have sustained damage that cannot be reversed or undone. Things cannot be put back the way they were. Apologies, financial retribution, and acts of kindness will never truly return what was stolen. How can you ever be repaid for time lost, a love stolen, or any other type of unkindness or even abuse? It's impossible. It is time to move forward and live in peace. And with God's help, you can do just that.

When you decide to bestow amnesty, you are not ignoring the fact that the offense took place—you are merely canceling the debt the offender owes you. You are taking control of your future and retrieving your happiness. You are refusing to allow another person to continue controlling your tomorrows. Herein lies great freedom. The perpetrator may never feel any sense of sorrow for their wrong, and they may never serve up amends, but your forgiveness bars them from having any control over you. From the point of forgiveness, your thoughts and actions will not be based on what they said about you or did to you—they will be a result of who you are.

DECEPTION: "IF I FORGIVE HIM, I WILL LET HIM OFF THE HOOK"

I recall a conversation with a lady who used to cut my hair. She knew I was a minister, and each time I went to get my hair cut, she would tell me about how her ex-husband had wronged her. She would go into great detail about his actions and the condition he had left her in; her anger was evident. Unforgiveness was robbing her joy and preventing her from moving forward. She had three young girls at home who needed her love and guidance, but bitterness bolstered her negative emotions. I always tried to be sensitive and minister truth to her. I encouraged her to think and speak more positive thoughts. Her unwillingness to forgive was wreaking havoc in her and in her family's homelife.

One time I asked her, "Why don't you forgive him and rid yourself of this anger and bitterness so you can go on with your life and create a home of solitude and peace for you and your children?"

"You want me to forgive him? I will never do that after what he has done to me."

While she was ranting, I was most concerned with the scissors in her hand, so I encouraged, "Stop and think for a moment. Is he having a hard time?"

"No, his life is going on. He is dating women and having a good time while I have to go to work every day. He does not care about me and what I have to do."

My response to her stormy ranting was, "Now just think for a moment. He is in control of your thoughts and feelings, yet he is having a good time. It isn't right for him to have done you the way he did and leave you in this present condition, but your anger and bitterness aren't affecting him—they are affecting *you*! He is moving forward, so who is controlling you?

Her retort was swift: "If I forgive him, I will let him off the hook, and he will get away without having to pay for what he has done to our family. I will be left holding all the problems."

I reminded her that she had the problems anyway, whether she forgave him or not. I encouraged her to forgive him so she could, once again, be free and creative. She expounded on the fact that she dwelled on ways to hate him day and night. She was constantly pondering ways to hurt and get even with him.

"Have you ever considered that your thoughts of hatred do not disturb him or change what he is doing?" I asked. "Not forgiving him is affecting not only you but also your three precious little girls and future relationships. Forgiving him will release you."

It took many return visits for her to finally see that her thoughts were causing her to self-destruct. Upon this revelation, she took on a positive attitude, and her days became filled with happy thoughts. She began to enjoy the people she met every day and opened herself up to the blessings of God on her life. All this happened when she truly forgave her ex-husband and relinquished the wasted thoughts about him. When her thoughts became pleasant, true happiness greeted her at the dawn of each new day.

What hurts are you holding on to? It is time to let go of the pain. The only way to begin this journey is to forgive. By beginning this process, you will free yourself. It all begins in your thought life and deciding to let go of the pain of the past. The longer you linger in the hope the offender will try to make things right, the longer you will live with the pain of the past. Disappointment and sadness will darken the days ahead if you hang on to the hurt and refuse to forgive.

I AM HURTING THEM AS MUCH AS THEY ARE HURTING ME

Hurting people hurt people. These self-victimized people wait for someone to step up and acknowledge their wrongs, but the wait can be too long and possibly will never come.

Your pain is not a crown to show off; it isn't a story that needs repeating. Rehearsing such thoughts poisons your soul. Holding close to the pain of the past is choosing to self-destruct.

I heard a story about a young boy sitting on a park bench. A man passing by stopped and engaged in a conversation with the lad. Noticing he seemed to be miserable, the man asked the little boy, "Are you in some kind of pain?"

The boy grunted, "Yes, sir, I am."

"Can I help you?"

Again, the young boy grunted, with a grimace of pain across his face. "No, thank you, sir; I'm sitting on a bumblebee. I think I am hurting him as much as he is hurting me."

Sadly, some people expend far too much time and energy trying to get even with the person who hurt them. If you are doing that, you may succeed in hurting them, but this does not undo the offense—it only deepens the wound inside you. Even more tragically, some decide to take their revenge public and tell the story in the hope of stacking humiliation upon the offender. This retribution may bring momentary satisfaction, but it will never right the wrong the person has endured. If you take this route, such tactics will only cause more aggravation and friction in your life, even a chain reaction in other areas of your life.

The best and only solution: forgive. Let it go and relish in the freedom that will soon come your way. Think yourself into taking action right now, right where you are. Let the love of God reign supreme within you, ask for His help, and do the right thing. Love the enemy or loved one, whichever it may be, and be the bigger person. Jesus said it this way:

"But I say to you, love your enemies, bless
those who curse you, do good to those
who hate you, and pray for those who
spitefully use you and persecute you."
MATTHEW 5:44

I have witnessed people fight, hurl hate-filled words, and take action that only made matters worse. Nothing was accomplished except an extension of hurts on both sides. Life is short. When someone causes hurt to invade your space, practice Philippians 4:8 by *thinking* on things that will give you life. Choose to live every moment with peace and happiness.

Finally, brethren, whatever things are true,
whatever things are noble, whatever
things are just, whatever things are pure, whatever
things are lovely, whatever things are of good
report, if there is any virtue and if there is anything
praiseworthy—meditate [think] on these things.
PHILIPPIANS 4:8

Do your best never to allow the actions of others to gain control over your thoughts. Take control in the battlefield of your mind. Forget any notion of retaliation or payback. Hanging on to those desires will only waste your time, hinder your growth, and bring sadness and frustration into your future. Hurting someone will never fix what has been done to you. Don't allow yourself to be brought down to their level, thus causing you to miss out on His peace in your life. Do not let your unwillingness to forgive delay your Creator's blessings on your future. Harboring bitterness is detrimental to your happiness.

Dear friends, never take revenge. Leave
that to the righteous anger of God. For
the Scriptures say, "I will take revenge; I
will pay them back," says the LORD.
ROMANS 12:19 NLT

At one time or another, we have all been hurt or betrayed by someone, but we cannot afford to let that one moment in time become so big in our lives that we think and talk about it all the time. This just results in giving strength to the pain. I see many people hanging on to a wrong that someone has done them and living their daily life through this hurt. Once wounded, they tend to always see life through this event and experience the resulting pain over and over. Many blame their current circumstances on other people. A better approach is to think about your future and what you desire. You may have been knocked down, but you can get back up. Will you continue to allow those who hurt you to control you through your unforgiveness? What God has for you is much greater than what has happened to you. Happy thoughts will set you on the road to recovery.

Therefore let us pursue the things
which make for peace and the things
by which one may edify another.
ROMANS 14:19

Peace comes with giving our lives to Jesus; it is forever our greatest encounter in life. Nothing will ever rival

His compassion for us. From this moment on, choose to focus on Jesus and His love for you—and not on what has happened to you in the past.

LET IT GO!

Some people keep a book of remembrance of their collection of *wrongs* compiled. They rehearse these conversations in their minds and build a Broadway play that seemingly never ends. When someone offends you, it is your choice whether to maintain control over what is replayed in your mind. Compounded anger will cause you to lose control of your emotions. Suddenly, thoughts of vengeance will permeate your soul. Redundant thoughts of this kind only hinder your future.

Forgiving someone does not always mean you want them to be part of your life again. It means you have dismissed the pain and refuse to carry those wounds into tomorrow. We have no do-overs but simply a heart of forgiveness. When you forgive, you remove the power for them to hurt you any longer. Until we forgive, we are prisoners of the person who has offended us. Forgive those who have insulted, attacked, or belittled you or taken you for granted. Even more importantly, forgive yourself for allowing them to hurt you.

When you forgive, you remove their power to control your thinking, weigh heavily on your emotions, or affect your decisions. Forgiveness offers you freedom. You can conquer evil with your good thoughts, which promotes positive actions. When the offense comes, you have a choice to make. Whose domain will you allow to be established in your life? The thoughts you esteem, the actions you take, and the words you speak will bring life or death.

Beloved, never avenge yourselves, but leave the
way open for God's wrath [and His judicial
righteousness]; for it is written [in Scripture],
"VENGEANCE IS MINE, I WILL REPAY," *says the Lord.*
ROMANS 12:19 AMP

Dear friends, never take revenge. Leave
that to the righteous anger of God. For
the Scriptures say, "I will take revenge; I
will pay them back," says the LORD.
ROMANS 12:19 NLT

Leroy Satchel Page was a famous baseball player who was an incredible pitcher and the first African American to be inducted into the baseball hall of fame. He faced criticism and racial slurs yelled at him from the stands, but he never let those taunts get to him. He said this: "Work like you don't need the money. Love like you've never been hurt. Dance like nobody's watching."[2] He had learned to keep his thinking and emotions in the right place.

IS PROVING OURSELVES "RIGHT" THE IMPORTANT ISSUE?

Several years ago, Sharon was struggling with some major changes taking place in her body. She became very sensitive and emotional, which was not like her at all. I tried to be compassionate, even though I didn't understand the physical dilemma she was facing. During this time, we were vacationing at a majestic place on the ocean's shore; our view was impeccable. Our time together was so enjoyable. On a particular day, after spending an especially

---

2   Paige, Satchel. Quoted in "Satchel Paige Quotes," BrainyQuote.com: https://www.brainyquote.com/quotes/satchel_paige_390217.

peaceful time together worshipping the Lord and having our devotions, we embraced and felt amazing as we kissed each other, ready for the day.

A short time later, we were driving in the car, and everything was going just right. I spotted an Italian food store off the side of the road and said, "On the way back to our room, I would like to go in there and see what they have."

Sharon replied, "You have been in that store."

"I most certainly have not!"

"You most certainly have!"

This banter continued back and forth, each of us maintaining our ground and position until all at once my tone changed. Turning the volume up, I insisted, "I have not been in that store!"

Matching my increased volume, she responded, *"Don, you have been in that store!"*

Of course, I had to go to my *volume control* and amp up my level even more. *"I don't care what you say. I have never been in that store!"*

We all know what her response was.

At that moment, I recognized that our day was not going to go as we had planned if something did not change right then and there. I quieted myself for a few minutes and let my emotions subside. I then said, "Sharon, my darling, if you say I have been in that store, well then, I have been in that store."

She looked at me and, with a beaming smile, took my hand and said, "I love you, Don Clowers!"

Being *right* at that moment was not what was important. Having peace with my love and enjoying the day far outweighed *being right*.

You may think I compromised and took the easy way out. No, I knew she was going through things she had never dealt with before, and I needed to be sensitive. Years later, we both look back at that incident, and she still believes she was right. I *know* I was right.

We do not always have to be *right*. Bigger issues are at hand—happiness to embrace and joy to walk in. Let go and decide to think yourself happy!

CANCEL THE DEBT

Unforgiveness is a sin. It is an ongoing way of thinking that goes against everything the Bible teaches us.

> *For if you forgive others their trespasses [their*
> *reckless and willful sins], your heavenly*
> *Father will also forgive you. But if you do*
> *not forgive others [nurturing your hurt and*
> *anger with the result that it interferes with*
> *your relationship with God], then your*
> *Father will not forgive your trespasses.*
> MATTHEW 6:14–15 AMP

Refusing to forgive is choosing to self-destruct. Christ forgives us when we come to Him; we, in turn, are instructed to forgive others. Jesus gave a brilliant depiction of a debt being *forgiven* as well as a debt being *held onto*:

> *"Therefore the kingdom of heaven is like a*
> *king who wished to settle accounts with his*
> *slaves. When he began the accounting, one who*

owed him 10,000 talents was brought to him. But because he could not repay, his master ordered him to be sold, with his wife and his children and everything that he possessed, and payment to be made. So the slave fell on his knees and begged him, saying, 'Have patience with me and I will repay you everything.' And his master's heart was moved with compassion and he released him and forgave him [canceling] the debt. But that same slave went out and found one of his fellow slaves who owed him a hundred denarii; and he seized him and began choking him, saying, 'Pay what you owe!' So his fellow slave fell on his knees and begged him earnestly, 'Have patience with me and I will repay you.' But he was unwilling and he went and had him thrown in prison until he paid back the debt. When his fellow slaves saw what had happened, they were deeply grieved and they went and reported to their master [with clarity and in detail] everything that had taken place. Then his master called him and said to him, 'You wicked and contemptible slave, I forgave all that [great] debt of yours because you begged me. Should you not have had mercy on your fellow slave [who owed you little by comparison], as I had mercy on you?' And in wrath his master turned him over to the torturers (jailers) until he paid all that he owed. My heavenly Father will also do the same to [every one of] you, if each of you does not forgive his brother from your heart."

MATTHEW 18:23–35 AMP

The king in this parable represents God. The servant who had his debts forgiven represents anyone who has been forgiven of his or her sin. The second servant is anybody we have not yet forgiven for hurting us. We are still holding on to their offense. It may be that they have abandoned or rejected us and we feel we have the right to hold on to this offense because of how deeply they hurt us. Jesus was very clear: forgive them or you will stay in your prison of bitterness.

THINK ABOUT WHAT JESUS DID *FOR* YOU—NOT WHAT SOMEONE ELSE DID *TO* YOU

If you evaluate the extent of your hurt only by what has happened to you, instead of what Jesus did on the cross, you will erroneously feel as though you are rewarding your enemy if you forgive them. But when you consider the enormity of forgiveness at the cross, you can offer forgiveness to others so you are free from bitterness and resentment and on a path to a happy and fulfilled life.

> *But God demonstrates His own love toward us, in that while we were still sinners, Christ died for us.*
> ROMANS 5:8

When God forgives you, you are set free from your past. As a believer, you now have been empowered to extend to others the very thing that has been so generously given to you. Now forgive and be free.

> *Let all bitterness and wrath and anger and clamor [perpetual animosity, resentment, strife, fault-finding] and slander be put away from you, along with every kind of malice [all spitefulness, verbal abuse, malevolence]. Be kind and helpful*

to one another, tender-hearted [compassionate,
understanding], forgiving one another [readily and
freely], just as God in Christ also forgave you.
EPHESIANS 4:31–32 AMP

People who have been forgiven by God, through Jesus Christ, understand what God has given them but often struggle with actually letting go and choosing to forgive, just as they have been forgiven. Sometimes they mirror the forgiven person in the parable. When the master forgave him, he did not have the same willingness to forgive the one who owed him.

As believers, we should continually pray for right thoughts to rule our minds and judge everything we do in the light of what Jesus did for us. Thinking about how our heavenly Father has always treated us will be a reminder to treat others the way we desire to be treated.

When you think God's way, you will understand that you are not forgiving the other person because they *deserve* it. You are forgiving them because God forgave you when you didn't deserve it.

Love is a decision. Our ability to forgive is based not on feelings but on a decision and resolve. Our decision to forgive is made by faith, despite how we feel. Although we may never feel like forgiving, our commitment to God and obedience to His Word are based not on feelings but on a desire to fulfill His will. Forgiveness will become a way of life for the person who wants to do things God's way and chooses to think on good and lovely things.

How can you know you have forgiven someone? If you have truly let the offense go, when you hear their name mentioned or see them, you will have no feelings of resentment toward them. You will be at peace around them.

Learning how to forgive is a process. You may not feel like forgiving someone, but remember, forgiveness is a decision, an act of love. It is a step of faith. You need to make a deliberate choice to forgive and then trust God to help you follow through.

In the past, after I had forgiven—or thought I had—I would sometimes tell others how this person had offended me. I didn't realize that by doing this, I was influencing them to think badly of the one who had offended me. I was not acting in love—I hadn't completely let go of the resentment.

If, after choosing to forgive, you find yourself telling others about it, ask yourself why. Have you really forgiven them, or are you still clinging to the offense? If you have forgiven, you shouldn't still be talking about it. Forgiveness is putting it away as if it had never happened. That does not mean you will be able to forget. You will remember what they did to you, but you will not have bad thoughts about them. You will want no harm to come to them, and you will pray for God's best for them. First Corinthians 13 says love will not give attention to a time of suffering wrong.

Some have asked me, "Should I go to the person who has hurt me and tell them I have forgiven them?" I think in most cases this would do more harm than good. Remember, forgiveness is for you, not the offender. Why tell them unless they ask you?

I recall a gentleman who approached me and said, "I want you to know I've forgiven you. You offended me once." When I asked him how I had offended him, he told me that was no longer important to him. I was shocked because

I assumed I had always been kind and thoughtful to this person. Now I had to keep myself from feeling offended. He had learned to forgive me and move on, and this was the right thing for me to do as well. I would not have had to struggle with this if he had never brought it up because I hadn't realized I had offended him.

REMEMBER JESUS

To be able to forgive, we must always be mindful of what Jesus did for us when He went to the cross. He took all our sins upon Himself and forgave us all. If we keep rehearsing over and over what has been done to us by someone else, we lose sight of what He did on the cross for us.

If you struggle with unforgiveness right now, please contemplate how Jesus fully forgave you. You and I were not worthy of His forgiveness, but He bestowed it on us willingly. We can choose to forgive willingly because of His life inside us.

> *When God our Savior revealed his kindness and love, he saved us, not because of the righteous things we had done, but because of his mercy. He washed away our sins, giving us a new birth and new life through the Holy Spirit.*
> TITUS 3:4–5 NLT

Chapter 6

Discontentment

Content or discontent. Which *tent* do you live in?

We live in a society where multitudes of people are searching for contentment. Merriam-Webster defines *contented* as "feeling or showing satisfaction with one's possessions, status, or situation."[3]

People pursue many avenues to find contentment, looking for more possessions, a higher status, or a better situation. Cunning advertisers try to capitalize on this need by claiming what they are offering will make you happy, content. Happiness is "just around the corner," they boast. But happiness is not right around the corner, or in your next purchase, or the latest gadget. It's not even in that pay raise . . . or a better job . . . or gaining popularity . . . or even fame. If you are a follower of Christ, it is inside you.

> *I have learned how to be content with whatever*
> *I have. I know how to live on almost nothing or*
> *with everything. I have learned the secret of living*
> *in every situation, whether it is with a full stomach*
> *or empty, with plenty or little. For I can do*
> *everything through Christ, who gives me strength.*
> PHILIPPIANS 4:11–13 NLT

---

3   Merriam-Webster, s.v. "contented," accessed February 2, 2023, https://www.merriam-webster.com/dictionary/contented.

What a statement penned by the apostle Paul. He had found true contentment—in the Lord. As long as we look for someone or something else to provide our contentment, we will never achieve it. I know many are perpetually searching for contentment, but it always seems to elude them because they are seeking it in all the wrong places. Things, money, fame, and notoriety will never bring the contentment Jesus offers us.

We can get stuck in our own little world of discontentment when our thinking turns to *if-only*.

If only I had a different job, my life would be different.

If only I had a different spouse, my life would be stress-free and nag-free.

If only I had a better car, my friends would respect me more.

If only my house were grander, I would be satisfied.

If only my clothes were more fashionable and carried the proper label, I would be more cultured and accepted.

When you live with this *if-only* mindset, you may finally get those things you thought would make you happy, only to find yourself still discontented. You purchase that new, *must-have* car, only to find out the new car scent is short-lived. Then, technology updates on the next year's model make your *if-only* purchase obsolete. It doesn't matter what you achieve in your pursuit to have the *if-only* because that satisfaction is short lived at best. Contentment achieved that way is a vapor that quickly dissipates.

ABUNDANCE CANNOT BRING CONTENTMENT

We all deal with discontentment in life from time to time. Every one of us has looked in the mirror and said, "If only..." Even King Solomon, the wisest of all men who ever lived, found himself discontented. Take the time to read Ecclesiastes 2:1–11. The Lord had asked him to request anything he desired, and Solomon asked for wisdom. Because he asked for wisdom instead of riches, wealth, or power, God bestowed all those things upon him, including wisdom. But the Lord warned him to be careful and not allow these other things to take precedence over his desire for wisdom. Solomon flourished and excelled, but soon found himself wanting more and wallowing in discontentment. Even though the Lord had lavished Solomon with more than he had even asked for, it wasn't enough. One wife was not enough. He ended up with over seven hundred wives and three hundred concubines. *Oh my*, where was his wisdom there?

Once Solomon started down that road of discontentment, he found himself chasing contentment outside of God. *Bigger and better* became his goal to fill the daunting void caused by his own discontentment. He built houses, gardens, vineyards, and ponds of water. He possessed an abundance of male and female slaves, flocks, and countless herds. The Bible tells us he increased more than *all* who had preceded him in Jerusalem, and he did not refuse his eyes anything they gazed upon. If Solomon wanted it, he got it.

You may think a man like Solomon, the ruler of a nation, unprecedented in wealth, power, women, and houses, would finally get to the point where he had *enough* and could just be content and happy. The Bible tells us all those luxuries he sought *profited him nothing*.

People buy bigger homes, fill them with extravagant things, and drive cars they can't afford, thinking these things will bring them their much sought after contentment—but they don't. They want it, get it, and then don't want it anymore. Then a house in the mountains or a European vacation lures them in. They always reach for something else—ever seeking satisfaction, but never achieving it. Contentment and happiness are never found in *things*.

I love living in a beautiful home and driving nice cars, but my point here is that *things* will never make us happy or content. The more we get, it often seems, the more we want. The vicious cycle is never-ending.

I recently talked with a man who owns several large, expensive homes across the country. He said it was nice to have all those homes, but once acquired, he had to maintain them, hire people to take care of them, and pay taxes and insurance on them—all to enjoy each one only a few days a year.

I have traveled to many nations of the world, often ministering to people with no financial means whatsoever. I have taken helicopters into villages so deep in the bush that people had to walk an entire day to attend a meeting. There was no running water there, no indoor plumbing, and often, a simple mud hut was their only abode. The ceiling height of these humble homes was usually not even high enough to stand upright. Yet I soon realized they experienced more contentment and happiness than people who *think* they have everything.

DISCONTENTMENT BREEDS COMPLAINTS

Discontented people tend to complain. The word *complain* means "to find fault; . . . to make an accusation; bring a formal charge."[4] Complaining only makes things worse. However, positive thinking opens the door for the Holy Spirit within you to bring knowledge, wisdom, and revelation and guide you in your next steps.

Continually contemplating good thoughts will lift you to a heaven-ordained perspective. Regardless of how life tries to mess up your path with stumbling blocks, continue steadfast in your pursuit of thinking good things based on your trust in Jesus. Cheerfulness lifts your perception, which ultimately is your reality.

When at your place of employment and things are not going well, if you complain about your situation, its ugliness will likely be magnified. Begin to vent your negative sentiments to others and watch the issue grow at a pace that soon grows out of hand. Faultfinding and a critical tongue will always serve you up a portion of problems that are far from palatable.

Do to others as you would like them to do to you.
LUKE 6:31 NLT

Godly thinking will help you maintain cheerfulness in unpleasant situations. It will allow you to not just survive but also thrive in the land of happiness and success. Godly thinking will help your creativity to flourish. Jesus will help you solve problems, open doors of opportunity, and draw people who are like-minded into your domain.

---

4   Collins English Dictionary, s.v. "complain," accessed February 2, 2023, https://www.collinsdictionary.com/us/dictionary/english/complain.

For the despondent, every day brings trouble;
for the happy heart, life is a continual feast.
PROVERBS 15:15 NLT

A NEGATIVE ATTITUDE TRAVELS WITH YOU

Sometimes you may have to change your job, your church, or your relationships because they have run their course. That is just part of life, and it's important to have a positive attitude about getting started in new places. But if you leave those seasons because you are discontent, offended, angry, or upset and hope to find greener pastures elsewhere, you will enter your next situation the same way. You will still be discontent. When leaving one place for the wrong reasons, you can rest assured that all those thoughts and feelings will be awaiting you at your next destination. Find contentment where you are right now if you desire new doors of opportunity. When you find contentment, you can easily follow God into better employment, relationships, places of worship, and other facets of life.

Once I was speaking on this subject in a service. As the meeting concluded, a man approached me. He was contemplating an opportunity for a better paying job and was ready to vacate his present employment to embrace this new opportunity. He felt he was being mistreated where he was currently employed and realized it was time to move on. He shared with me, "Because of your message, I am not sure if I should leave or not." He explained his situation, stating that he felt his boss was not treating him with the respect he deserved. In fact, his boss was giving him such a hard time he felt he could no longer remain there.

I asked him, "How do you know things will be any better where you are going?" I cautioned him he may face the same kind of situation or the same kind of boss in the new place he was contemplating.

He responded, "I don't know, but it's very difficult where I am." I encouraged him to look for the good points in his present place of employment and think about those things. I asked him to consider what the Bible says concerning working for someone else:

> *Work with enthusiasm, as though you*
> *were working for the Lord rather than for*
> *people. Remember that the Lord will reward*
> *each one of us for the good we do.*
> EPHESIANS 6:7–8 NLT

Any place you work, you should do so as though you are working for the Lord. This will help you be more responsible and do a much better job because you are not doing the job just to receive wages but also to please the Lord with your faithfulness and a good attitude. And with that comes contentment.

Others around you may be discontented, even grumbling. If you will do your best on the job and have a good attitude, even though others may not, you keep God on your side to help you.

You may ask what this has to do with your happiness. If you are unhappy at work and are just enduring it, dwelling all day on negative thoughts, you will not be happy after leaving work for the day. I encouraged this man to have a talk with his supervisor and explain to him that he wanted to do a good job and please him. He did that, telling his boss he was there to make his job easier, and that with his boss's help, he believed his productivity and performance could improve. Their discussion had good results.

The man went back to work with a new mindset and soon found that he and his supervisor had a much improved working relationship. His newfound energy and enthusiasm for his work brought some positive changes. His supervisor was overwhelmed by the new productivity. It wasn't long until this man got a promotion and a raise. Several years have passed since that conversation, and he has enjoyed many improvements and increases in pay and benefits.

Whether you are discontented with your job, a relationship, the place you live, your church—or whatever—don't make a change expecting things to be better.

If you are not content and happy, do a self-examination and, with Jesus' help, make the corrections needed to change your thinking. Then follow up with the steps of action necessary to put you on the path of contentment and happiness right where you are. Remember, contentment and happiness begin with a thought.

HAVE PAINFUL EXPERIENCES BROUGHT DISCONTENTMENT?

What painful experiences have you had in life? Have you suffered from a failed relationship? Have you lost a good job? Have you been rejected by someone you loved? Have you been passed over for something you desperately wanted? When that event occurred in your life, how did it make you feel? What did you think at the time? How did you respond to the situation? Did you complain and get discouraged?

Did you doubt God? Did you allow the experience to leave you in a constant state of discontentment?

I hope not. I hope you thought good thoughts and gave God praise during the ordeal. But if not, you can still redeem that failure by allowing it to motivate you to respond differently in the future. Your negative thoughts didn't improve the situation, did they? They actually made the situation worse. When bad experiences come your way (and Jesus promised they would in John 16:33), you have no choice but to endure them. Whether you want to or not, you have to navigate the storms of life. But you can derive benefit from those storms if you choose to walk through them in faith, not defeat.

I will tell you this: the bad experiences Sharon and I have had in life have made us better, not bitter. Both my wife and I have learned through each bad experience that we had no control over those events, and that God did not bring the *bad* into our lives. Think about this: bad things over which we have no control will happen to us, even as godly people. Remember, the true secret is to *think right*, and, while you are experiencing the worst of the situation, God will give you His best to walk through the storm. Every trial has a self-limit. Robert Schuller said, "Tough times never last but tough people do."[5] When tough times come, *think yourself happy*.

ONLY ONE WAY TO FIND CONTENTMENT

Only in Jesus can we find the contentment we tend to seek from the world's order. He stands in wait to give us all the desires of our hearts.

---

5   Schuller, Robert H. Quoted in "Robert H. Schuller Quotes," BrainyQuote.com: https://www.brainyquote.com/quotes/robert_h_schuller_156000.

Contentment is inside you, not to be discovered outside. If you cannot find contentment in Him, you will never possess it. No one person, or even an abundance of things, will make you truly happy. Many pastors and leaders never find true contentment because they compare their ministry and finances with others. They compare the size of their congregations with that of their peers. They try to mirror another minister's approach, or try to emulate their particular *formula;* hence, they choose to relinquish contentment.

Contentment is an inside job. We need to emulate the sentiments of the apostle Paul when he proclaimed that whatever state he was in, he was content. And his circumstances were often anything but easy. He was hated, beaten, and unjustly arrested. He spent years in prison but hadn't broken any laws. His secret? I encourage you to read the entire fourth chapter of Philippians. It will reveal much of Paul's mindset. Some of his thoughts found there . . .

Rejoice in the Lord always.

Be gentle to everyone.

Remember, the Lord is near.

Instead of worrying or being anxious, pray about everything.

And here is that scripture we've already talked about:

> *Finally, brethren, whatever things are true,*
> *whatever things are noble, whatever*
> *things are just, whatever things are pure, whatever*
> *things are lovely, whatever things are of good*
> *report, if there is any virtue and if there is anything*
> *praiseworthy—meditate [think] on these things.*
> PHILIPPIANS 4:8–9

Contentment is a learning process that begins with how and what you think and proceeds by what you say and how you act.

If you are discontent, an honest self-assessment of your thought life and what shapes it will help you discover the problem—you. This is empowering because it gives you the power to change. Change your thinking—and change your destiny.

Chapter 7

Grief: Dealing with Loss

Continued grief comes from holding on to things you no longer have.

Any kind of loss is difficult to deal with. Eventually, all of us will have to deal with some type of loss in life. (In the next two chapters I will discuss grief suffered because of divorce or betrayal and grief from the loss of a loved one in more detail.)

Some losses are monumental, while others deliver less of a sting. But they all hurt. Even King Solomon, the wisest man who ever lived, understood that loss is a natural consequence of living in this world. Here are a few of his words about seasons in life . . .

A time to gain, And a time to lose, A time
to keep, And a time to throw away.
ECCLESIASTES 3:6

It is much easier to walk in gain and keep something good than it is to know the anguish of loss and deal with it, but both are inevitable parts of life that come in seasons.

Amid pain and loss, questions loom large. Anxiety about how to cope seems to grow out of control. The presence of anxiety is unavoidable, but the prison of anxiety is optional.

You may have experienced the loss of a loved one through disease or from natural causes after they lived a long, fruitful life. Perhaps a life-changing injury of a close friend has presented itself to your life and, try as you may, no acceptable answer as to *why* can be found. Still others suffer from a congenital birth defect that will haunt them as each new day dawns.

Some have known all too well the four D's of life: divorce, death, disease, and difficulties. Amid these storms, there is seemingly no shelter suitable to outlast the gales that pummel. A loss of any type can be difficult to bear.

FINANCIAL LOSS

One type of difficulty that affects many, especially in today's volatile economy, is financial loss. Maybe you have lost a home to foreclosure, a business to bankruptcy, a car to repossession, or an investment to the ups and downs of the stock market. People suffer loss in many forms and to various degrees.

Loss of some kind is a very real part of life, and none of us is exempt from its grip. This is not a negative pronouncement; it is just a plain and simple fact of life. We will all, at times in our lives, come face to face with loss, and the way we deal with that loss will shape our future. We can look to ourselves or others for the answers. Or we can choose to allow God to be the prevailing force amid the fray. He makes all things possible and loves us unconditionally. God is an ever present help, but only if we rely on Him and His Word during our time of pain.

God is our refuge and strength, always
ready to help in times of trouble.
PSALM 46:1 NLT

A monetary loss is difficult, but it is not the end of the world. Nearly every day we hear news of global disasters that have left people homeless because of floods, fire, or storms. Some have lost everything they had ever accumulated but give thanks that their lives were spared.

In no way am I trying to diminish the pain of losses people have realized. You may be experiencing a tragedy right now. Sudden loss can bring a shock to all your senses. Life is good, and abundance is prevalent; then calamity comes calling, and the shock of it all crashes in. Without warning, these catastrophes invade our peace, and we have to deal with the aftermath.

I have compassion. I am not trying to be lighthearted about such events, but I do know the Lord is present to help us cope. Handling your loss begins with your thoughts. It is natural to grieve when you have any kind of loss; however, there comes a time when you have to accept it and move forward. Some find this easier to deal with than others, but deal with it you must. Your faith must rely on the power of the Holy Spirit, who lives within you. Starting over from loss is not easy, but it is possible. "If you can believe, all things are possible to him who believes" (Mark 9:23).

If you believe the loss is too severe and devastating for you to start over again, more than likely you are grieving and holding on to that which is no longer there. I urge you to hear me: After loss, things change. Without peace, inner conflict makes it difficult to stand up and move on. Find comfort in the Holy Spirit. His comfort will bring peace and strength to rise above misfortune. Your trust in Him will guide you through the most turbulent times. You cannot rise up *physically* until you rise up *on the inside*.

The scripture says in Micah 7:8, "When I fall, I will arise; When I sit in darkness, The Lord will be a light to me."

FOCUSING ON JESUS OPENS THE DOOR TO PEACE

The grieving process after a loss will give way to the healing process when your thoughts and focus are on Jesus. Refuse to allow bitterness to set up camp in the province of your mind. Don't let the *why* dominate your thought patterns. You must move past the pain and rise above the circumstances.

You can *give up* or *get up*—the choice is up to you. Rising up spiritually and emotionally will help you understand how you can go about rebuilding your life. If you do not *get up* in your thinking, chances are you will never rise up at all. Many choose to feel sorry for themselves and live as *victims*.

I know a Christian couple in Florida who lost everything in a hurricane. Their business had been flourishing. They lived in a beautiful home. But then a hurricane wiped out all they had built. There was no insurance to replace their home or business, and suddenly they found themselves living in a tent with only the food strangers provided for them. Life was swiftly altered; the misfortune was mind-blowing. However, they decided that no matter how difficult and painful the process would be, they were going to get up and rise above their current situation. They decided that getting up was better than giving up. First, they *got up* in their thinking and believing by encouraging each other that God would somehow help them—and He did.

Seeing this couple today, you would not discern any remnants of the pain and loss they encountered. They focused on God's goodness and how He had spared their lives. There is no trace of a victim mentality; instead, they have chosen to be victors. Today, they are far removed from their tragedy, with a prospering business and a beautiful home. They sowed *seed* into the kingdom, but it all started with their thought life. Their decision to trust in Him empowered them to build life once again.

You can allow fear to overcome you and keep you chained to devastation . . . or you can hope in God. You can focus on grief, become overwhelmed with fear, and let anger and bitterness rule your life . . . or you can place your trust in Him alone. Someone may have done you wrong, spoken evil about you, or tried to bury you with falsehoods; this pain is real. You must overcome evil with His goodness, darkness with His light, and suffering with His joy.

Be mindful of your thoughts. Stress will be magnified if you do not control them. Negative thoughts will rob you of your peace and cloak the answers the Almighty has for your life's next chapter. He does care for you, and His plans for all of your tomorrows are good. "'For I know the plans I have for you,' says the LORD. 'They are plans for good and not for disaster, to give you a future and a hope'" (Jeremiah 29:11 NLT). When you suffer loss, your emotions run the gamut, but you can speak out of His Word of Truth and seize control of your mind.

If you lock your thinking on what has happened and never move past the grief, your emotions will weigh you down with a heaviness that makes you feel trapped. Do not rehearse the darkness over and over in your mind; this will only serve to cause the pit of despair to grow deeper. Control your thoughts, or they will control you. Losing your job could be a blessing in disguise, as heaven has orchestrated a much grander plan for your life. Think differently. Remember, grieving is holding on to what you no longer have.

Many people who have walked through these kinds of bitter experiences will tell you that the presence of the Lord can be very real, despite the momentary darkness. They will also tell you that although life will never be the same, that doesn't necessarily mean that life will be worse. In time, things may be even better than they were before because life's darkest moments have a way of strengthening us and helping us better define our priorities and goals. The way a person comes through this kind of trauma has more to do with the person's thoughts about a situation than it does the actual circumstances.

IT'S A CHOICE

Some losses are worse than others. While all of us dread losing a job or a pet, some among us have lost a child or the use of one or more limbs. Some have lost their sight or hearing. Some have lost everything they had built over a lifetime. Many have lost marriages they desperately wanted to save. And there are those who have lost their reputations because of foolish mistakes or misguided decisions. Often these self-inflicted losses are the most difficult to overcome.

The way we choose to deal with the losses we incur will have a profound impact on the quality of our lives. It may have a profound impact upon eternity as well, because the difficult seasons of life, not the easy ones, reveal our hearts and our true character.

Rest assured, God can be an unwavering source of strength whenever we face the bitter cruelties of life. In fact, in the Old Testament, David described the Lord as his "refuge and strength, A very present help in trouble" (Psalm 46:1). He boldly proclaimed that the Lord had "delivered [him] out of all trouble" (Psalm 54:7).

David knew about life's sorrows and losses. At various times in his life, David lost his freedom, an infant child, his third-oldest son, and the respect of his family and subjects. In addition, his actions as king caused the deaths of at least seventy thousand people in a terrible plague inflicted on Israel as a direct result of David's decisions. So, he was well acquainted with loss and grief, but he also knew how to get through his grief with God's help.

Many of God's people in this present generation do not know how to deal with loss. They don't even recognize loss as a valid part of life. God is not the one who causes or brings the loss, but life happens. The Bible says in John 10:10 that it is the thief (Satan) that comes to kill, steal, and destroy. So always remember, when you lose something, don't blame God. Keep your thoughts focused on Him for guidance and direction. Trust Him to help you move on. The prophet Isaiah said it well: "You will keep in perfect peace all who trust in you, all whose thoughts are fixed on you!" (Isaiah 26:3 NLT).

If you watch the news on television, you know that almost every night, there's a story about people like you and me who have suffered far greater losses in their lives than the ones we have known. Due to a terrible storm, a sudden flood, a devastating fire, an unannounced tsunami, or some other type of natural or manmade disaster, these people suddenly lose everything they have, including their homes and businesses. And yet when a reporter sticks a camera in their faces, most often we hear, "Thank God; we're still alive!"

Obviously, losing something of value can be a painful and disruptive experience, particularly if the thing is irreplaceable. Only the people who have been through this kind of tragedy can fully understand what it is like. A shock factor is involved that lets you know immediately that your life won't ever be the same. And the thing that makes this kind of experience devastating is the sudden and unexpected manner in which it occurs. This morning, everything was fine; this afternoon, everything is gone.

I understand the traumatic impact a life-altering loss can have on a person and a family. I am not approaching this serious matter in a cavalier way. I have had my fair share of losses too, and I know that once I walk through the natural processes of grieving, there is hope on the other side. The air never smells sweeter than immediately after a storm. But I also know I cannot exit the grieving process unless I have the right kind of thinking during the storm and immediately after it.

Obviously, we need to mourn. As I have explained, that is a natural human need for a time after experiencing loss. You may not always smile and feel happy when you are suffering, but after a reasonable amount of time, a healthy-thinking person should be able to move beyond any loss. He should be able to rise from the ashes and to regain his strength. The journey to victory begins when the storm first hits. It begins with proper thinking.

If you believe the loss is too severe and you will never be able to recover, you are right. But if you believe you can rebuild your life and God can restore what you have lost, you are right again. You will be able to overcome this setback and climb back to where you were—perhaps higher. You will have what you believe you will have, and you will become what you believe you will become. *This is why your relationship with the Lord should be more important than anything else in your life.* This is why you must choose to think proper thoughts the next time you suffer a serious loss.

BETTER THINKING

So how do we think the right kinds of thoughts when disaster strikes? How do we handle loss the way God wants us to?

First, a person who has suffered a significant loss must deal with his natural grief by finding peace for his soul. Peace is not the cure-all for the problem of lingering grief, but it certainly is the best place to start the healing process. Without peace, a person's inner conflict can make life seem too painful to ever enjoy again.

> *Don't worry about anything; instead, pray*
> *about everything. Tell God what you need, and*
> *thank him for all he has done. Then you will*
> *experience God's peace, which exceeds anything*
> *we can understand. His peace will guard your*
> *hearts and minds as you live in Christ Jesus.*
> PHILIPPIANS 4:6–7 NLT

So, the next time you find yourself grieving over a tremendous loss in your life, find the comfort of the Holy Spirit. Let God's presence begin to heal and restore you. Trust in Him, even if you don't understand why He has allowed this tragedy to come your way. Worship Him and thank Him for helping you and loving you through it.

MOVING ON

King David was not a perfect man. He made many mistakes and sinned against God during his life. Nevertheless, God favored David and elevated him highly because he was a man after God's own heart (Acts 13:22). One reason for God's favor was the fact that David trusted in God even when he could not understand the losses in his life.

David's first child with Bathsheba was a little boy, and this infant was struck with a terrible illness that threatened his life. For a solid week, David prayed to the Lord and fasted. He lay on the ground and asked God over and over to spare his son's life, but after seven days, the baby died. This scripture tells what David did next:

So David arose from the ground, washed
and anointed himself, and changed his clothes; and
he went into the house of the LORD and worshiped.
Then he went to his own house; and when he
requested, they set food before him, and he ate.
2 SAMUEL 12:20

David knew personal loss that was just as deep and just as inexplicable as most any person's loss. But he also knew how to keep things in perspective. Once the child was dead and there was no way to change the outcome, he refused to hold God, himself, or anyone else responsible. He refused to wallow in self-pity. Instead, he went to the house of the Lord, and he worshiped. Then he got something to eat, and he continued with his life.

I'm not saying that David did not feel any pain—he obviously did. David was not living in denial; he knew the child had died, and he knew what this meant for him and his wife, but he decided to think rationally about the situation. He chose to move on with his life, which still had purpose despite his tragic loss.

Too many people never move on. Too many people constantly dwell on the things that have happened to them in the past and continue living in a state of grief. Don't allow this to happen to you. Don't allow anger or bitterness to fill your heart. Don't allow questions of *why* to take over your mind and eat away at your soul like a cancer. From your limited perspective and with your finite understanding of God's infinite creation, you will never fully understand why things happen the way they do or why God allows them to happen. But you can trust that God loves you unconditionally and will help you through.

YOU HAVE CHOICES

What choices will you make when life deals you a blow? You may choose to start living in a perpetual state of self-pity and develop a *victim mentality* that reshapes the way you perceive yourself, God, and others, as well as the way you live out your remaining days on this earth. Let me repeat, you don't have to live with a victim mentality. God will give you the strength and courage to get up if you will not cling to the pain of what has happened to you. Learn to think about the things that make you happy instead of those that make you sad. Don't keep rehearsing the loss over and over in your mind.

God has never promised us that bad things won't happen. Bad things have happened throughout history, even to His most faithful servants. But God has promised to walk with us through these brutal experiences, and He has promised to help us rebuild after life's devastating storms. In fact, two entire books of the Bible—Job and Nehemiah—are devoted exclusively to the subject of restoration and to the demonstration of God's grace in our lives following the calamitous events He allows.

It is so important to be mindful of your thoughts. If you don't take control of them, especially during the bad times, you can easily allow bitterness and unbelief to take root in your heart, eventually making you a bitter person your family and friends won't even recognize. Negative thinking seasoned with anger and self-pity can rob your peace and joy and detract you from the fulfillment of your destiny. It can destroy your relationships and even your health. It can leave you bitter and lonely as the years go by.

If you lock your thinking on what has happened and never move past the grief, your emotions will weigh you down with a heaviness that makes you feel trapped. Do not rehearse the darkness over and over in your mind; this will only serve to cause the pit of despair to grow deeper. Control your thoughts, or they will control you. Losing your job could be a blessing in disguise, as heaven has orchestrated a much grander plan for your life. Think differently. Remember, grieving is holding on to what you no longer have.

Guard your thoughts. Don't allow false expectations of life to cause you to mourn excessively, and don't allow the natural inclination to blame yourself or others to make you sour or cause you to spiral into a black hole of despair. Instead, rejoice in all the good things God has given you.

Keep a right perspective; remember that things are only temporary. Only your relationship with the Lord is *forever*. So, thank God when *things* come and thank Him when *things* go. Trust Him to fill every void suffered through your losses with something even better and more delightful. Be a better person as the result of your loss, not a bitter person filled with pain. Remember that what you think is what you feel. Think on the things that will give you joy and happiness.

As mentioned earlier, in the next two chapters, I will discuss two specific causes of deep suffering and grief: divorce and other kinds of betrayal . . . and the death of a loved one.

Chapter 8

Grief: Facing Divorce

I have never experienced the pain, loss, rejection, or grief of divorce. It has been said that the pain of divorce is more severe than losing someone to death. Only the people who have experienced both would truly know or understand. The pain of divorce is epic for both husband and wife, but it also affects so many others around them. Mothers, fathers, children, in-laws, and friends all bear the brunt of this all too common tragic experience.

Often children are involved, thus complicating the situation even more. During the process, it is common for the children to become frightened, insecure, and so entangled with the process that it takes them years to recover. Many bear undeserved guilt for causing the divorce.

I have been closely involved with divorced friends and family as they try to pick up the pieces of their broken marriage and life. It takes a toll on everyone. My heart cries out for anyone who has endured such pain.

In some cases, the lives of the divorcees and others close to them are changed forever—they never get over it.

Too often one parent tries to alienate children from the other parent by putting innocent kids in the middle of the battle. They manipulate the situation, using the kids to gain an advantage or usurp control. This kind of parental selfishness is beyond sad because of the deep emotional wounds it inflicts on the children. Grieving over the pain and loss of a relationship, as well as possibly losing the respect of their children, is not easily overcome. The pain is real.

Some people very close to me are children of divorced parents. Many of them have become angry and bitter and live with unforgiveness. They feel abandoned. Blaming their parents causes them to continue in an unfruitful, negative life. Of course they are hurt, but as long as they blame a parent, they cannot heal. This is only an excuse to live in denial. They refuse to accept that they have a problem themselves that prevents them from going on with their lives. They refuse help from anyone and continue to think negatively about everything. Even though the divorce was not caused by the children, as they grow older, they have to take responsibility for their thoughts and actions. If they don't, they will live sad and unproductive lives.

I have watched people close to me try to continue hurting their divorced spouse, rather than go on with their new life. Instead of thinking right thoughts, they spend much of their time trying to destroy each other's peace and happiness. Their thoughts focus on their pain and trying to get even. They don't realize what they are doing to themselves as they allow the divorce to minimize their future and keep them in a prison of pain and control.

These individuals continue holding on to the broken pieces of yesterday and cut themselves daily with the same old broken pieces. It would be much better to choose to forgive and wake up to a new day saying, "Today is the first day of my new life, which will be better than ever."

BURIED FEELINGS NEVER DIE

Are you still grieving over a divorce, either yours or your parents'? Are you holding the pain inside?

Don't hold your feelings in. As long as grief remains on the inside, the pain remains very real and damaging. What you *think on* becomes your reality. This kind of pain, loss, and rejection distorts your judgment in future relationships. You will never be free and happy until you can allow yourself to let go of this grief. Maybe you don't know how to let it go. Your thoughts may convince you that you have been wronged and judged unfairly.

Jesus knows the feeling of being wronged: "He was despised and rejected—a man of sorrows, acquainted with deepest grief. We turned our backs on him and looked the other way. He was despised, and we did not care. Yet it was our weaknesses he carried; it was our sorrows that weighed him down" (Isaiah 53:3–4 NLT).

Jesus suffered unfair pain and sorrow. He understands what you are going through. The Lord not only understands it but also desires to help you through this disaster. The word *through* is one of the most powerful words in the Scriptures. He brings us *through* the wilderness and valleys.

> *Even when I walk through the darkest valley, I*
> *will not be afraid, for you are close beside me.*
> *Your rod and your staff protect and comfort me.*
> PSALM 23:4 NLT

Through is His plan for your future. He took your sorrow and pain. He nailed your grief to the cross, and He understands your pain. Give all to Him; do not stuff it inside you.

WHERE IS YOUR FOCUS?

If you continue to focus on how you've been wronged, that's what you will think about. That's what you will talk about. Those thoughts can lead you to anger, bitterness, and unforgiveness. We've already talked about how unforgiveness can destroy your life. It may even lead you to take your own revenge on the one who has hurt you. I urge you not to let that happen. Remember, the unforgiveness is hurting you much more than it is hurting your spouse (or parents). Ask Jesus to help you let it go!

> *Since God chose you to be the holy people*
> *he loves, you must clothe yourselves with*
> *tenderhearted mercy, kindness, humility,*
> *gentleness, and patience. Make allowance*
> *for each other's faults, and forgive anyone*
> *who offends you. Remember, the Lord*
> *forgave you, so you must forgive others.*
> COLOSSIANS 3:12–13 NLT

Perhaps it's fear that has gripped you. Your thoughts center on what lies ahead for you—financially, socially. That can be paralyzing. Remember that your spouse's provision is not your source. Jesus is your source. And He wants to show you the way, to provide for your needs. The only way to take your focus off fear is to remember that Jesus loves you unconditionally and has promised to provide for you. But you need to trust Him. To let the Holy Spirit show you the way.

> *Do not be anxious or worried about anything, but*
> *in everything [every circumstance and situation]*
> *by prayer and petition with thanksgiving,*
> *continue to make your [specific] requests*
> *known to God. And the peace of God [that*

peace which reassures the heart, that peace]
which transcends all understanding, [that
peace which] stands guard over your hearts
and your minds in Christ Jesus [is yours].
PHILIPPIANS 4:6–7 AMP

You may be dealing with guilt. In Chapter 9, we will discuss more fully how you can overcome feelings of guilt. Those feelings of guilt may or may not be justified. Perhaps you are a child of divorced parents and blame yourself for the divorce. No matter what you think you did or didn't do, your parents—not you—are responsible for their choices. Perhaps your spouse left you and you feel if you'd been a better spouse, you'd still be together. Or perhaps you betrayed your spouse and now feel guilty about that. As long as you let the guilt haunt your thoughts, you will not be able to move forward. And there is only one way to get rid of it. Talk to Jesus. Tell Him what you did wrong. (He already knows but wants to hear it from you.) And then ask His forgiveness. He died on the cross so your sin can be forgiven. Believe He has forgiven you . . . and then forgive yourself. Depending on the circumstance, the Holy Spirit may or may not lead you to go to the one you wronged to seek their forgiveness as well.

If we confess our sins, He is faithful and
just to forgive us our sins and to cleanse
us from all unrighteousness.
1 JOHN 1:9

Other kinds of negative thoughts may be preventing you from working through your grief and moving on. I am not making light of any of this. I know the pain is real, and I know taking these steps will take courage. But I also know

Jesus is bigger than the pain and is waiting to help you. He loves you unconditionally. He cautioned that in this world, life would bring us pain, but He also promised to be with us and help us through it.

DON'T STUFF IT

If you are burdened by grief and pain, admit it. Do not stuff it or pretend it is not there. You cannot move on from the place where you are until you can admit where you are. You may have lost your whole family and many friends. This loss is real and painful. Accept the fact that you are human, with human emotions. You don't want to carry this pain for even one more day. It is time to move on. Ask God to help you with your thought life. He will heal you *through* this painful process. The apostle Paul said it this way: "I focus on this one thing: Forgetting the past and looking forward to what lies ahead" (Philippians 3:13 NLT).

If you desire to be happy again, *you can*. Paul said, "I think myself happy." This is the choice you must make. God is a good God, and He has good things in store for you, regardless of your present circumstances. Begin to plant happy thoughts in your mind. This is not idle daydreaming—good thinking and productive thoughts will open the avenues of your soul so the Holy Spirit can bring healing to your emotions. Your relationship may or may not be restored, but God will restore *you* and help you to be whole and happy once again.

Let your *comeback* be *greater* than the *setback* you've experienced in life. Don't let someone who has given up achieving happiness or fulfilling their dreams cause you to give up on yours! What God has for you *is for you*.

Think and meditate on God's promises for you. Lift your head, stand tall, walk in victory, and know that you are an *overcomer*! Your failures cannot dictate your future unless you hand it over to defeat! *Hold on* to God's Word and believe what He says about you!

Whatever you refuse to feed will eventually starve and die. When you dwell on past hurts, you drag them into the present and relive them again and again. Leave the past by choosing forgiveness!

Get up every day and get your soul happy by thinking about everything God has in store for you—and let the rest of your life be the best of your life.

Chapter 9

Grief: Experiencing the Loss of a Loved One

No matter how strong a Christian you may be, or how much faith you have, at some point, you will lose a loved one. This is not a pessimistic view; it is simply a fact of life. We are sojourners here on this planet, and one day it will be our time to move on to eternity.

My wife and I lost our fifteen-year-old son, Jeff, to accidental death. Our entire family felt the pain of this traumatic event. Sharon and I have each lost both of our parents—a very difficult fact we had to face, but we had to let them go. We have lost them in this life. We take solace in the hope that we will reunite with them when our time on earth is fulfilled.

Having lost loved ones, I know what it is like to experience intense grief. With the initial impact, the first emotion is pure shock. You know they are gone, but it is hard to incorporate this into your psyche because only yesterday they were here with you. Family and friends gather around you; love and support come in like an avalanche. Phone calls commence, flowers arrive, cards and thoughts of condolences abound. God's strength comes to help you try to cope with a future without someone close. The flow of sympathy and compassion helps you face the next day's rising sun.

THE LORD MADE THIS DAY

I will never forget the first morning after Jeff's death. I woke to face the reality that our son was gone, knowing I would arise to this reality every day. I knew we would have to return to the funeral home with the clothes he would be buried in. This was an excruciating time, and in my prayer time with the Lord, I struggled to find the words to speak. I was not angry with Him. I did not blame Him. In the shower, a song welled up within me: "This Is the Day that the Lord Has Made." As tears ran down my face, the song in my heart sprang forth. I sang and spoke words that had *life*. I was experiencing the pain of death, and I knew I had to feed my soul with thoughts of His goodness and allow the Holy Spirit to overcome my emotions and fill me with strength.

Even though I did not feel like singing, I made a conscious choice to do so. Singing this song did bring the inner strength I needed in my soul. You too can find your way by deliberately deciding to think thoughts of Him and make choices that honor Him, despite the terrible position you find yourself in. This is what the apostle Paul decided when he said, "I think myself happy," although he had been falsely accused and was facing prison . . . and eventually, death.

I prayed and at times would break down and cry. This gave me strength for the next step I would have to take—the drive to the funeral home. Beyond my own grief, witnessing the pain Sharon was experiencing as we picked out our son's casket was overwhelming. This only served to escalate the pain I was already trying to deal with myself. I cannot forget this specific moment, the anguish and pain I was feeling, and yet, even then, the joy of the Lord was strengthening me. His power in this inner turmoil was beyond words. *My feelings* were not joyful, but *my spirit was*, for I had the *joy of the Lord.*

Thinking the right thoughts opens the floodgates of heaven and allows His strength to fortify your soul. You can choose to live in pain and be overcome with grief, *or* you can ask God to give you His strength in your time of need.

LAUGHTER IN TIMES OF GRIEF

I do not know how I could have coped with the grief without the Lord to rely on. The funeral was an exceptionally difficult, emotional experience. Even though our son's memorial service was upbeat and only positive things were spoken, the ride in the funeral procession to the cemetery was poignant. As we peered through the windows of our vehicle, the emotions and thoughts of the people attending seemed overwhelming to us. When we arrived at the burial site, the finality stared us down, but with the comfort of the Holy Spirit, we got through it.

I will never forget the hustle that greeted us when we arrived back home from the service. Food had been catered and delivered; some of those who attended the funeral had gathered. As the evening progressed, very dear friends and relatives from out of town lingered and conversed. While I visited with some of our guests in one room, Sharon did the same in another room. We both went from room to room and engaged in conversation, seeking solace from those around. Everyone did their best to keep upbeat and talk about everyday life. Sometimes the conversation and laughter became boisterous.

Laughter was not welling up on the inside of Sharon, our other three children, or me, but I knew it would bring healing to our souls. Some of the stories became quite hilarious, and the anecdotes offered lightened the rooms. My mind at times thought, *This is not right*, but the laughter was a healing balm and good for everyone gathered. "A cheerful heart is good medicine, but a broken spirit saps a person's strength" (Proverbs 17:22 NLT).

Our hearts were wounded, our strength had waned, but the laughter was medicine to our souls. We did not feel like laughing; it did not take away our pain, but the happy thoughts helped. "Laughter can conceal a heavy heart, but when the laughter ends, the grief remains" (Proverbs 14:13 NLT).

We laughed, we socially engaged, but as the scripture says, when the laughter ended, the grief remained. All this proved to be an operation we had to complete. Finally, the guests departed, and only our immediate family remained. Although we were all together, loneliness crept in because the one we were grieving for was now absent. We prayed, cried, embraced, and comforted one another before turning in for the night. It was a sad, long night, but I continued to pray, think positive thoughts, and encourage my family. This consistency would prove important for each one of us in the days to come.

> *Weeping may endure for a night,*
> *But joy comes in the morning.*
> PSALM 30:5

Our weeping covered a span much longer than a single night, but we knew our morning would come, even if it was not the next morning. Psalm 30:5 lets us know that while there is weeping during the dark times and bad situations, the nighttime darkness will eventually pass. Then it promises that the dawning of a new day will bring joy that will supersede yesterday's grief. No two people are exactly alike; for some, their nighttime grief seems like an eternity, but for others, it is a brief encounter. Each of us processes things differently, but God promises all of us joy as we look to Him.

We wept because of our loss, yet we had joy inside despite our collective pain. The joy of the Lord truly became our strength. This may not make sense to you, but you must understand that our faith was in God, and we knew we could come through this with His help. Joy is not a feeling; it is a byproduct of the fruit of the Spirit. We knew God loved and cared for us, and His joy sustained us through our grief and pain.

But the Holy Spirit produces this kind of fruit
in our lives: love, joy, peace, patience, kindness,
goodness, faithfulness, gentleness, and self-control.
GALATIANS 5:22–23 NLT

God and His Word are unchanging; His promises are available to you this very moment. The more you focus on the promises of God, the sooner the morning's joy will overtake you. It is of great importance for your life that the joy coming from God's love is not merely a *feeling* but also provides the strength and power to deal with your pain. Some are emotionally stronger than others; however, if you will embrace the Holy Spirit and meditate on His goodness in the darkest hours of pain, He will be there for you to experience the joy of the Lord.

I talk to people who are angry with God and blame Him for the loss of their loved one. Blame never helps anything or anyone. It only keeps you in a state of confusion, turmoil, and pain. Being angry with God will not bring back the one who died. All it does is keep you locked in a prison of grief. If you are angry with Him, please let it go. By being angry, you are living life through that anger, and you will never move on until you decide to release it.

Embracing the goodness of God sustained me through my darkest hours. The joy of the Lord was my strength when I didn't have it on my own. His comfort gave me the courage to face the unbearable pain within me. I am not denying that I was hurting or pretending there was nothing wrong, but His help enabled me to face each new day.

LETTING GO OF THE GRIEF

Many years ago, I watched my precious mother-in-law, Mary, suffer and almost grieve herself to the grave. Her son Timothy was killed in an automobile crash. He was attending the University of Buffalo in Buffalo, New York, and lived with his parents in Niagara Falls, Ontario, Canada, and commuted each day.

His neighbor and friend who lived on the same street also attended the university and rode with him each day. He was also killed in the car accident. An intoxicated driver got in the wrong lane and hit them, taking both their lives instantly. This was a heartbreaking day for both families.

My mother-in-law was waiting for Timothy to come home that day. It was his twentieth birthday. She had a surprise birthday party planned for him and was so excited. She could hardly wait to see his reaction to the surprise. Time passed, and he never came home. Finally, she received a call telling her that her son and his friend had been killed in an automobile crash.

This news was so shocking and unbelievable, she screamed, "No, this cannot be true; this has to be a mistake!" Sadly, it was true. She writhed with pain and grief. However, details had to be taken care of. It was almost more than she could bear, but she managed to get through making the necessary arrangements. She struggled through the funeral and burial, which brought the reality home to her that he was really gone. He was no longer alive on this earth.

Soon after the funeral, the phone calls stopped, the flowers died and were discarded, and the cards quit coming. Even though she had a husband, three other children, and three grandchildren, the loss of her son was so difficult to process that Mary spent most of her time grieving. She was so sad every day. It seemed to her that life was not worth living. She felt she could not smile because of her grief and pain.

Mary experienced even more pain because the person who took the lives of these two precious young men was never charged. He did not spend one day in jail, and he had no remorse for his crime. Neither did either family receive any kind of compensation from the drunk driver's insurance because two countries were involved. Of course, this would not have changed anything, but the injustice weighed on her mind.

A year passed after Timothy's death, and she seemed to be no better. We could see the toll the continual grief was taking on her. I repeatedly tried to encourage her but to no avail. She would attend church regularly but did not get into the service. She just kept grieving. Since this happened several years before our son Jeffery was killed, my wife and I had not yet experienced that kind of loss and pain. However, I knew somehow that my mother-in-law had to get through the grieving process and go on with her life or she would remain miserable.

I would hug her and pray for her, but she was stuck in her pain and grief. One time after I finished praying for her, I could see it was still not helping. I looked into her eyes and spoke with authority: "Mary, you must get on with your life. You did not die—Timothy did—and you must let him go. He is with Jesus, and you will get to be with him again in heaven. Each day, think about what you still have. Think about him being in the presence of God. Make each day count. Begin to train yourself to think better thoughts. Think about how you had Timothy for twenty years and how wonderful it was. Think about what a kind and gentle person he was. Pray and ask God to help you let go of this terrible grief and think of the joys of life instead of only the pain you are experiencing. Remember how Jesus took your grief and pain on the cross."

> *But [in fact] He has borne our griefs, And*
> *He has carried our sorrows and pains.*
> ISAIAH 53:4 AMP

Mary took my advice and began to change her thinking process. Each day she prayed and started thinking on good things. Then, little by little, she began giving more attention to her other three children and her grandchildren. She found out that she could enjoy them even though she had suffered such tremendous loss. Her life started changing for the better, and within just a few months, she was *thinking herself happy*. Life became sweet again as she put God first every day. Once again, she found life to be enjoyable, living with the Holy Spirit's comfort. She never forgot her son but learned how to think better and live as God intended her to. She has now passed on to glory and is in heaven with Timothy.

Grieving over the death of a loved one is a normal process; however, the longer you grieve, the more difficult it becomes to return to normalcy. I know people who continue to grieve because they think it keeps them close to their loved ones. However, continual grieving only delays the healing process and does not keep you close to the one lost. Your loved one has passed from this life into eternity, and only your memories keep him or her close to your heart.

THE *WHY* AND *IF* QUESTIONS

Have you lost someone dear to you?

After the memorial service, family and friends go back to their normal lives. When the flowers dry up and fade away, when the phone calls cease, you are faced with the reality of your loss. Even though loved ones surround you, there is a big void on the inside that brings sheer loneliness. This is one of the hardest parts of the grieving process. At this point, you have to choose to either go on with your life or stalemate in the grieving process.

Moving on from grief to healing begins with your thoughts. If you have suffered any kind of loss, make a conscious decision to move forward. If you do not decide to *go on,* you will remain stuck and feel sorry for yourself. Then the *why* questions will begin their assault on your mind. Your thoughts may run rampant. *If I had only done this,* or *If I hadn't done that, I could have prevented this terrible event from happening.* As long as you entertain the *whys* and *ifs,* grief and guilt only tighten their stranglehold on you. The *why* and *if* thoughts change absolutely nothing and keep you in a dark cave of despair.

The *why* and *if* dilemma, when dealing with our son's death, consumed my thought life for a while. However, I decided not to stay there. When these questions come, they bring their accomplices, *self-blame* and *guilt*. Blaming does not change what has happened, and it never helps with closure or moving forward. It took me little time to recognize the *why* and *if* as a lethal combo that I could not allow to set up residence within my heart. I loved my son and I would have done anything to keep him from harm's way, but we cannot predict the dangers that can arise in any given situation.

You may have dealt with issues concerning doctors, medicine, hospitals, or the like, and in the midst of it all, made the best decision based on the circumstances and information at the time. However, your best may not be enough to avoid tragedies that lie in wait. You cannot change the past. You cannot relive that opportunity or moment ever again. Thinking about what you could or could not have done is an exercise in futility. Instead, choose to think thoughts that will give you life and strength.

> *"Today I have given you the choice between life and death, between blessings and curses. Now I call on heaven and earth to witness the choice you make. Oh, that you would choose life, so that you and your descendants might live!"*
> DEUTERONOMY 30:19 NLT

The only way to come through the healing process is to choose life in your thoughts. If loss and death have already come knocking on your door, they have delivered an unwanted package you never signed for. Reflecting on what you could have done differently cannot change what has happened.

I recently spoke to someone who had suffered a death in their family. They were haunted by the *why* and *if* questions in their minds. I encouraged them, "Do not let those two questions keep you trapped, thinking about something you cannot change." Negative thoughts do not fade away on their own; you must decide to put them away.

DON'T ASK *WHY*

A few days after I lost my son, the great missionary statesman T. L. Osborn dialed my number. T. L. had experienced the personal pain of losing a son; he could easily empathize with the plight of my mind. We had a common bond—a mutual understanding of the pain death brings.

His call—timely. His words—encouraging. His sympathy—comforting.

He told Sharon and me, "Don't ask God *why*." He went on to say that if you ask the Lord *why*, you may or may not receive an answer. If you do receive an answer, you may not like it, and then you are just asking God for an argument. He encouraged us to leave this *in God's hands*. He said, "Jeff is gone and nothing can bring him back, but you and Sharon now must move on with your lives." Even though we did want to know *why*, the encouragement from this man of God proved to be reassuring.

We heeded T. L.'s advice and decided to move ahead. We still did not understand the *how* and *why* of what had happened, and the emotional pain was still prominent, but we had to move forward. Sharon and I worshipped the Lord, we prayed, and we gave the entire situation and tragedy to Him. This approach helped us cope and deal with the negative and painful thoughts that hurled themselves against us. This helped us get our minds off the pain and allow the Holy Spirit to comfort us as we began the steps to take back our lives.

MYRIAD EMOTIONS

If you have lost a loved one, I am sure you have experienced many different emotions. They don't go away just because a few days, weeks, and months have passed. You have to *choose* to think happy thoughts.

One of the emotions both my wife and I had to deal with was guilt. Why guilt? As we decided to go on with our lives, that meant we would start to enjoy life again. We would be doing something normal with friends or family and enjoying what was taking place when all at once the negative thoughts came—we should not be enjoying this moment. We learned we had to get rid of these thoughts as soon as possible according to 2 Corinthians 10:4–5 (AMP):

> *The weapons of our warfare are not physical [weapons of flesh and blood]. Our weapons are divinely powerful for the destruction of fortresses. We are destroying sophisticated arguments and every exalted and proud thing that sets itself up against the [true] knowledge of God, and we are taking every thought and purpose captive to the obedience of Christ.*

Guilt can be very challenging to overcome. Each day we had to renew our thinking. It took months to get over the guilt and, even now, years later, those feelings sometimes creep up and have to be put away.

If you have lost someone close to you through death, I encourage you to leave the *whys* and *ifs* behind, because they only bring more pain. None of our family got through the loss quickly, but each day, we did our best to rebuild a normal life. We knew Jeffery was not coming back. Understanding we would meet him again in heaven did not take away the pain, but it did help. We did all we knew to do to go on with our lives and ministry. I spent a lot of time in prayer, and Sharon spent many hours listening to worship music and meditating on the goodness of God.

We still had three wonderful children who needed us, and we needed them. Life was never the same again, but we all had our ways of dealing with the loss. It took time because there were things like his birthday we had to face without Jeffery. The next big event was Thanksgiving, and we would have to celebrate it without him. This was a tough one, but we made it through.

Then Christmas came six months after he had passed. Jeffery was not there anymore for us to buy him his favorite gifts. This was a very sad time without him, but once again, we called upon God's strength to help us get through. Each day, we tried our best to let go of the grief and pain and look forward to our future, knowing that one day we would be united with him in heaven. We would talk about him from time to time and remember his kind and tender heart and how grateful we were to have this wonderful son for fifteen years. Talking about him was a great relief for us as we remembered the good times we had together. We reflected on some of his great personality traits and the fun things we did with him. Oh, how we missed him.

We did not stay home for our first Christmas without him. We went to be with Sharon's family because we felt this would be a better place for all of us to be together. Sharon's mother, Mary, understood our pain because she had gone through the same loss with her Timothy.

On Christmas Day, as we sat at the table with everyone and all the wonderful food, we tried to enjoy the moment, but it was very difficult to do. At one point I had to excuse myself from the table and go to another room to shed tears. This seemed to help, and then I went back to the table. Not a lot of words were spoken. We were all remembering Jeffery and dealing with the fact that he was not there. However, each of us encouraged the other, and the day was not a total loss as, with God's strength, we climbed another mountain.

DON'T GET STUCK IN THE GRIEF

As we prayed and decided we were going to live again, we started getting better each day, but there was still a numbness that is difficult to explain. *Sharon and I decided not to stay stuck in grief.* However, there remained things we had to face—one of them was the anniversary date of his death. We did our best, trying not to hold on to the bad memories of that dreadful day. God gave us the grace and comfort to get through it—another hurdle we had to face in our healing process. Even though we had to face these difficult times each year, I will tell you that it did get better with time because we chose not to dwell on and think about the loss. Instead, we directed our focus on the fact that God was our hope and strength.

We had wonderful friends in ministry who were so encouraging to us. Our church family was loving and there for us. I am grateful to all who shared their love and time with us. Our church families were so compassionate and did their best to show us how much they loved us. Some days were good, and others were not as good. But as time passed, the bad days got further and further apart. God's love and kindness helped us to continue forward. Instead of becoming bitter, I let the pain help me to become a much more compassionate person and minister.

As a pastor, I have ministered in many memorial services since the loss of our son. At first, it was very difficult for me because I would remember that day of Jeff's memorial service. However, it got easier as time passed. God gave me peace beyond my understanding (Philippians 4:7). I repeat, our loss helped me to have more compassion and understanding for the ones I helped with the memorial service for their loved one. "He comforts us in all our troubles so that we can comfort others. When they are troubled, we will be able to give them the same comfort God has given us" (2 Corinthians 1:4 NLT).

I have shared our story many, many times, in over fifty countries—not to call attention to our loss, but to let people know we have had to deal with loss just like other people. Being ministers didn't make things any easier. We did our best not to let the bad things outweigh the good. We chose to get up when tragedy came into our life. I encourage you to get up, no matter what you have faced. You can think yourself happy if you desire to go on with your life.

GRIEF CAN BRING ANGER

Whether a person experiences loss through death, divorce, financial disaster, or something else, remaining in grief opens the door to far too many negative thoughts and deadly emotions. Anger is one of those negative emotions you can choose to either entertain or dismiss. It begins with a negative thought—this is why I have belabored the point in going into much detail about the experiences my family and I have faced, even including my thoughts and feelings. When anger tried to come in, I chose to let it pass because I refused to be angry with the Lord or anyone else.

Some people were aware of the potential danger in the surroundings where our son was killed. If someone had taken the responsibility to fix the dangerous environment, our son would not have died. My wife and I could have chosen to be angry or point the finger of blame, but I knew this would not bring our son back. Choosing the path of blame and staying in the prison of anger would have only prevented me from moving forward. It was difficult enough to live with what had just happened to our son without adding anger, blame, and bitterness. Sharon and I decided not to become bitter. Instead, we chose His peace and moved forward with the Lord.

The tendency to want to quit ministry was there, but we decided we were going to express more compassion, love deeper, and give even more of ourselves to God and others. Thinking happy thoughts in the midst of our pain gave us great comfort. Yielding to these happy thoughts helped us take the right actions, move forward, and discover healing from grief, guilt, anger, bitterness, and pain.

Walking through this devastating event was not easy. When life dealt this blow, we knew we were not the only ones who had faced such tremendous loss and hardship. We had to choose to either walk through it or give up. Giving up must never be an option. Lester Sumrall once said that the greatest key to success is, "Just don't quit."

I have known many people who have allowed their loss to occupy their thoughts and command their thinking, so much so that they became bitter and lost even more. Far too often, parents who have lost a child end up getting divorced because the guilt, grief, and blame become overwhelming. A faultfinding aura leads to destruction, as strife takes center stage.

Take time for self-examination and determine exactly what you need to do to move your life forward. As we have learned, continual grief opens the door to anger, bitterness, blame, guilt, and misguided thinking. These will only bring about unsound thoughts and result in wrong decisions. If you have suffered a loss or been hurt, decide right now that you have lost enough and been hurt enough. Enough is enough.

THERE IS LIFE AFTER THE DEATH OF A LOVED ONE

I have penned these pages concerning our loss and grief for one reason—to let you know there is life after the death of a loved one if you choose to ask God to guide you through. He has promised to never leave nor forsake us, and we know that is true. We have found His comfort so real, and I know you can too.

As you begin your journey in returning to normal life, there are a plethora of emotions you will have to deal with. Daily tasks such as being at work, driving down the road in your car, or even being in a church service are difficult. Then suddenly, without notice, grief slips in and causes your emotions to overwhelm you. When the floodgates of grief begin to overtake you, sometimes the best thing you can do is just go ahead and cry. Let the pain out, and in those moments, endeavor to recall some good thoughts. Speaking forth positive words, even while you are weeping, can not only help your pain but also build up your emotional strength.

As you try to resume a normal life, feelings of guilt may rise up inside, but you need to realize that life must go on. In these times you have to *get up* even though this can be most difficult. You will have moments when you simply do not want to move forward, and you will feel a sense of guilt for doing so, but you will need to be persistent and resolute in moving on.

> *And Nehemiah continued, "Go and celebrate*
> *with a feast of rich foods and sweet drinks,*
> *and share gifts of food with people who*
> *have nothing prepared. This is a sacred day*
> *before our Lord. Don't be dejected and sad,*
> *for the joy of the* LORD *is your strength!"*
> NEHEMIAH 8:10 NLT

This particular verse of Scripture has been a real comfort to me many times. I read it and quote it often as a reminder that the more I give to someone else when I am suffering from some kind of loss or pain, the stronger I become. Today my wife and I are enjoying life after going through such a tragic loss. Why? Because we chose to depend on the Holy Spirit, love God with all of our hearts, and *think ourselves happy.*

TAKE YOUR LIFE BACK

The Lord is the love of my life and always has been. During my grief, Philippians 4:8 was a constant comfort to me. I would think of others who were experiencing some kind of pain, then do my best to minister life and comfort to them. Even though the pain of my heart was prolific, the compassion I extended toward others helped take my thoughts off of my grief.

Often when my family and I were just trying to enjoy ourselves, even in the simple pleasures of life, guilt would rise up to cast a shadow on our joy. Sharon and I knew our children needed our love and attention, so we would push through our feelings of guilt and give our family the time needed. We would not allow guilt and grief to be our way of life. We were determined to be happy. Eventually, happy moments turned into happy hours, then happy days, then happy weeks, then happy months, and now happy years. Although we encountered great loss, we chose to be happy because God had given us the strength and courage to truly enjoy life once again.

Decide that you are going to take your life back by moving forward. I remind you again, take this moment and evaluate where you are in your life. Are you happy? Have you let things keep you from enjoying your life and experiencing God's joy? If so, decide that today will be your turning point. Take it one moment at a time, one hour at a time, one day at time, until you learn how to *think yourself happy*.

Chapter 10

The Most Important Step

In this book I have shared many truths that will enable you to think yourself happy. Truths that will help you overcome fear and anxiety . . . worry . . . self-doubt . . . unforgiveness . . . discontentment . . . grief . . . and more. All these truths are based on the Bible, the Word of God. And they are all based on knowing Jesus Christ as your Lord and Savior. If you have never received Jesus as your Lord and Savior, I urge you to do that now.

Some call this step being saved or being born again or coming to faith. All these descriptions are accurate, but it's important that you understand it's not about religion. It's about a relationship with Jesus Christ.

The Bible tells us that everyone has sinned.

> *For everyone has sinned; we all fall*
> *short of God's glorious standard.*
> ROMANS 3:23 NLT

> *If we claim we have no sin, we are only*
> *fooling ourselves and not living in the truth.*
> 1 JOHN 1:8 NLT

That sin is a problem. God is perfect. He is holy. He loves us and wants us to live forever with Him in heaven, but there can be no sin in His presence. Yet we've all sinned. Perhaps we can get our act together and do good things? But that won't work.

> *For it is by grace [God's remarkable compassion and favor drawing you to Christ] that you have been saved [actually delivered from judgment and given eternal life] through faith. And this [salvation] is not of yourselves [not through your own effort], but it is the [undeserved, gracious] gift of God; not as a result of [your] works [nor your attempts to keep the Law], so that no one will [be able to] boast or take credit in any way [for his salvation].*
> EPHESIANS 2:8–9 AMP

God has provided a solution—the only solution. His Son, Jesus Christ, came to earth and lived a perfect life. Then He allowed Himself to be crucified—dying a death so painful we can't even imagine—to pay the penalty for our sin, yours and mine. Three days later, He arose from the grave, conquering death for us.

> *He made Christ who knew no sin to [judicially] be sin on our behalf, so that in Him we would become the righteousness of God [that is, we would be made acceptable to Him and placed in a right relationship with Him by His gracious lovingkindness].*
> 2 CORINTHIANS 5:21 AMP

Forgiveness is an undeserved gift from God. Jesus paid a great price in order to offer this priceless gift, but all we have to do is accept it. We do that by inviting Jesus to be our Savior and Lord.

We are made right with God by placing our faith in Jesus Christ. And this is true for everyone who believes, no matter who we are. For everyone has sinned; we all fall short of God's glorious standard. Yet God, in his grace, freely makes us right in his sight. He did this through Christ Jesus when he freed us from the penalty for our sins. For God presented Jesus as the sacrifice for sin. People are made right with God when they believe that Jesus sacrificed his life, shedding his blood.
ROMANS 3:22–25 NLT

Are you ready to take this step? In your own words, talk to God about it. Tell Him you believe these scriptural truths and need His forgiveness . . . that you want to receive Jesus as your Savior and to follow Him in your life. It's the most important decision you'll ever make—and by far the best one.

Chapter 11

Moving Forward

Are you ready to think yourself happy?

SURROUND YOURSELF WITH POSITIVE INFLUENCES

Positive influences are key to your development and growth. Saturate your mind and thoughts with *good* things by meditating on His Word, devouring Bible-based books, and listening to ministers who offer encouraging words from the Bible. Also listen to good music—especially worship songs that are edifying and help you think good thoughts.

Don't spend time associating with negative thinkers. The wrong companions will corrupt good character. These people have not grasped the concept of *what you think is what you feel*. These gloomy souls talk about their unfavorable feelings. They walk in the realm of *victim mentality*, always blaming others for their plight in life. However, as you surround yourself with people of good character and correct thinking, you will make great strides in owning Philippians 4:8. Making yourself accountable to godly men and women will help you reach your next level of spiritual maturity. "As iron sharpens iron, a friend sharpens a friend" (Proverbs 27:17 NLT).

GET PAST YOUR NEGATIVE EMOTIONS

To get past your negative emotions, you will have to take responsibility for your own feelings. Casting blame on others for how you feel, without taking responsibility, will only serve to justify your negative emotions. You own your feelings; you can change them if you desire to do so. The Almighty will give you the power to overcome, but you must want to change. In the course of my ministry, I have met many people who desire to change so their lives will improve; however, they don't know how to move past their negative emotions.

Changing your feeling begins with changing your thinking. This is something that only you, with Christ's help, can manage. It won't happen overnight, but you can change. The process of developing good thinking is like planting a seed. You sow the seed in the ground, you nurture the soil, and then, as time passes, you reap the harvest. In the same manner, you sow a thought and you get a feeling. A good thought will produce a good feeling, and a negative thought will bring a harvest of negative feelings.

> *The earth produces the crops on its own. First*
> *a leaf blade pushes through, then the heads of*
> *wheat are formed, and finally the grain ripens.*
> MARK 4:28 NLT

When you plant a seed of corn into the ground, after time a blade will emerge. Days later, the ear of corn begins to form. Soon after this, a full ear of corn manifests. The full ear of corn comes forth from one seed. It takes between 80 and 120 days before the corn matures and is ready to be harvested. This process of time is the principle of *seedtime and harvest* (Genesis 8:22). This is a kingdom principle and law of the harvest. The same holds true concerning the *good seed* you sow into the harvest of *good thinking* in your life. Trust the process. Practice good thinking—it will produce a beneficial harvest in your life.

The law of the harvest is found in Genesis 1:11. This passage of Scripture denotes that seed must produce after its own kind. You cannot reap tomatoes from a kernel of corn planted in the ground. This same principle holds true with regard to your feelings. If you desire good feelings, you must sow good, godly, pleasant thoughts. Change begins with the seed you sow. Bad thoughts yield bad feelings, just as good thoughts yield good feelings. It will take time to uproot the negative weeds in your life and replant the ground of your heart and life with good seed.

REFUSE TO BE CONTROLLED BY YOUR EMOTIONS

You are just a choice away from your new beginning—a new you. When you are serious about change, you don't need a new *year*—you just need a new *moment*. Sometimes, the best way to add to your life is to subtract from it. Those choices may seem hard, but the reward is His plan—and His plan is perfect. Just because you had some bad chapters does not mean that your story cannot end well. The past has had its time.

I read this quote from George Müller several years ago: "The first great primary business to which I ought to attend every day was, to have my soul happy in the Lord."[6] This quote had such a profound effect on me that I adopted

---

6   Müller, George. Quoted in "George Müller>Quotes>Quotable Quote," Goodreads: https://www.goodreads.com/quotes/703415-i-saw-more-clearly-than-ever-that-the-first-great.

it into my thinking and lifestyle. From that moment on, I decided to set this as a priority in my day and make sure my soul is happy before I attempt anything else lined up to face me that day. Making sure my soul is in a place of happiness gives me strength for the day and offers joy and peace, no matter what storms may rage.

At a recent ministers' conference, the host asked me to share insights from my many years of ministry. After more than sixty years of ministry, trials, and triumphs, this was an easy topic. My voice's trumpet was loud, clear, and concise; after all, I've lived and proven what I have believed for more than half a century.

My first explanation was that I have learned *not* to make emotional decisions because they can have serious consequences. In the past, I have made emotional decisions that paid painful dividends for extended times. I came to this conclusion: instead of asking God to make my emotional decision right, I ask God to help me make the right decision.

We make emotional decisions based on how they can affect us in the moment, but we have to capture the big picture and see how these choices will affect us in the future. Here is a word of sound advice: Let your emotions subside, and then decide. Make decisions that will help you enjoy life by keeping you on the path God has set before you.

Impulsive purchases and rash or brash decisions made on a whim are seldom correct in scope and have future consequences we can never foresee. A difficult encounter at the workplace may cause you to flare up and decide, "I've had enough of this place. I'm gone." Acting in such an emotional and irresponsible manner can leave you devastated and destined for regret. As a child of God, you must learn to turn your anger and frustration into something good, rather than letting them take you down a path of destruction.

People leave churches and abandon lifelong relationships because the most menial and trivial obstacles arise. Thoughts fester, emotions run the gambit, and hasty decisions cause permanent damage. No one is perfect. Life is a marathon, not a sprint. Seeing past the mistakes and flaws of others is paramount in relationships that were meant to last. Love is a decision, not a feeling. "Always be humble and gentle. Be patient with each other, making allowance for each other's faults because of your love" (Ephesians 4:2 NLT).

People make emotional decisions to suddenly marry. A brief courtship makes many emotions come to life and too often throws out God's plan and purpose. Because an emotional decision was at the helm of this voyage and a proper foundation and counsel were not sought, all too often it is not long before divorce lawyers are hired and hell springs forth. The happiness that should have been the foundation soon finds itself cast aside as emotions run rampant. Negative thoughts slay God-meant endeavors, thus stealing the happiness God had intended.

I remember back in 1962 when I first saw my beautiful wife, Sharon. The moment I met her, I was captivated and overwhelmed with extreme emotion. I will say this— they were good emotions. In the coming days and weeks, as we spent more and more time together, I realized this relationship was more than just feel-good emotions; we loved each other. We proceeded to get married, not only because we had good feelings toward each other but also because we were in love. Sharon and I both sought God's will and did not want to make an emotional decision. We did not want to go by our feelings.

Soon after, we married and began our journey together. We experienced and embraced the emotional journey but held our thoughts in alignment with God's Word. Three months into our marriage, we had our first big disagreement. I don't even remember the source of the conflict; we were both young and immature and letting our emotions control us.

At the time, I was leading a meeting in West Virginia. This disagreement caused us to not speak to each other for three days. We slept in the same bed, dined at the same table, and obliged each other by not speaking for three days. Our emotions were running rampant and controlled those three lonely days. Remember, emotions and feelings have no intelligence. We were captivated by the offense, and neither Sharon nor I wanted to take responsibility and make amends.

During my prayer time for the evening service on the third day, the Holy Spirit convicted me. I knew I had to apologize to Sharon. I had convinced myself she was wrong, but I knew I had to make things right. All the negative thoughts had to give way to righteousness. We loved each other. We knew love was a decision and not a feeling. My actions were hindering the Holy Spirit. I went to Sharon and made amends. She followed my lead and did the same. We learned from this mishap to not allow our emotions to control us when we disagree.

Love always wins.

REMEMBER THIS: IN EVERY CIRCUMSTANCE, GOD IS WITH YOU

I have contemplated the life of Joseph often over the years. Many close to him wronged him, but God had a plan. His story, found in the book of Genesis, is an exciting example of the sustaining power of destiny. Joseph was the eleventh of twelve boys in his family. In this large family, which consisted of four wives and thirteen children, Joseph was highly favored above all the other children by his father. However, when his brothers saw that their father loved him more than them, they hated him and could not speak peaceably to him. (See Genesis 37:4.)

This story goes on to portray so much more than a boy who was the favorite of his father. The story reveals to us the power of destiny. The Spirit of the Lord delivered destiny into the lap of Joseph in two dreams.

> *Now Joseph had a dream, and he told it to his brothers; and they hated him even more. So he said to them, "Please hear this dream which I have dreamed: There we were, binding sheaves in the field. Then behold, my sheaf arose and also stood upright; and indeed your sheaves stood all around and bowed down to my sheaf."*
>
> *And his brothers said to him, "Shall you indeed reign over us? Or shall you indeed have dominion over us?" So they hated him even more for his dreams and for his words.*
>
> *Then he dreamed still another dream and told it to his brothers, and said, "Look, I have dreamed another dream. And this time, the sun, the moon, and the eleven stars bowed down to me."*

So he told it to his father and his brothers;
and his father rebuked him and said to him,
"What is this dream that you have dreamed?
Shall your mother and I and your brothers indeed
come to bow down to the earth before you?"
GENESIS 37:5–10

Through these dreams, God revealed His plan and destiny for Joseph. A powerful future had been planned for him, yet much would happen to this simple man before he would realize his God-given destiny. Because of the dreams, jealousy loomed large in the hearts of Joseph's brothers as they plotted against him.

And when they saw him from a distance, even
before he came close to them, they plotted to kill
him. They said to one another, "Look, here comes
this dreamer. Now then, come and let us kill him and
throw him into one of the pits (cisterns, underground
water storage); then we will say [to our father], 'A
wild animal killed and devoured him'; and we shall
see what will become of his dreams!" Now Reuben
[the eldest] heard this and rescued him from their
hands and said, "Let us not take his life." Reuben said
to them, "Do not shed his blood, but [instead] throw
him [alive] into the pit that is here in the wilderness,
and do not lay a hand on him [to kill him]"—[he
said this so] that he could rescue him from them and
return him [safely] to his father. Now when Joseph
reached his brothers, they stripped him of his tunic,
the [distinctive] multicolored tunic which he was
wearing; then they took him and threw him into the
pit. Now the pit was empty; there was no water in it.
GENESIS 37:18–24 AMP

In a last minute ploy to spare his brother's life, Judah said, "What profit is there if we kill our brother and conceal his blood? Come and let us sell him to the Ishmaelites" (Genesis 37:26–27).

Potiphar, an Egyptian official, bought Joseph as a slave, but once again Joseph was clothed with favor. Soon, he was put in charge of everything in Potiphar's house. Things had slightly improved from the pit that once held Joseph, but he still was not walking in the manifested destiny God had ordained.

As time passed, Potiphar's wife became a seductress who desired more than Joseph's help around the house. She did her best to entice him into her bed, but Joseph refused to succumb to her temptation. Embarrassed and outraged, she cried rape, and soon Joseph once again found himself in the pit. It was a prison that had no resemblance to the destiny he had once dreamed of. (See Genesis 39:6–20.)

Even in these circumstances, the favor of the Lord was with Joseph, and soon he was ruling the prison. Destiny, although not yet realized, was still at work bringing Joseph closer to his fate.

When Pharaoh was unable to interpret a troublesome dream, he sought guidance. Joseph was summoned, and destiny began to take shape. When Pharaoh told the former prisoner his dream, Joseph not only interpreted the dream but also spoke of how Pharaoh should handle the circumstances and events that were to come. Before long, Pharaoh had placed his ring on Joseph's finger.

Shortly thereafter, Joseph was arrayed in the finest clothes. He was made the head of the whole nation of Egypt. Only Pharaoh held a higher position in all the land. Destiny had taken Joseph from the pit to the palace. And though he continued finding himself unfairly treated, God's Word assures us that God was always with him. In just one day, he went from being a common prisoner to an uncommon leader of the land. He took his place, fulfilled his dreams, and enjoyed his God-given destiny. God used him to keep His chosen people, the Israelites, alive through years of famine and more. Joseph later told his brothers, "You intended to harm me, but God intended it all for good. He brought me to this position so I could save the lives of many people" (Genesis 50:20 NLT).

Circumstances that may not be our fault are sometimes hurled upon us, and we bear the brunt of others' misdoings. When that happened to Joseph, he didn't feel sorry for himself; he battled with emotions, yet he refused to be limited by them. Joseph kept the vision God had given him years prior, rather than dwelling on the negative that had invaded him for years.

Never let *where you are* become *who you are*. Never view your future through the lens of your present condition. Refuse to allow circumstances to determine your expectations—never allow anyone to dictate the next chapter in your life. *You alone* get to pen those pages—make them epic.

> *For we are God's masterpiece. He has created*
> *us anew in Christ Jesus, so we can do the*
> *good things he planned for us long ago.*
> EPHESIANS 2:10 NLT

If you are going to live a happy life, you must learn to *see what you believe*, instead of *believing what you see*. Joseph saw the vision of what God had called him to be. He let his vision guide him, despite his present circumstances. Every trial has a shelf life. Winter ends and spring comes; the storm passes and peace unveils.

Some proclaim their faith in Christ, but they let anger be their persuading force. A sharp tongue is wielded with cutting blows as they lash out vile and wicked words of proclamation. Their trials with relationships, church, circumstances, and life plummet them into the depths of despair. How much of your life have you dismissed into oblivion by being angry or bitter against someone? Every one of these wasted moments lies in a casket that will never be resurrected, never retrieved.

Joseph decided not to be named in those ranks. He let good thoughts of hope, future, and promise permeate his life. At the age of thirty-nine, when he was ruling Egypt and his betraying brothers came to purchase food from him, he could have chosen to display anger, to get revenge. But no. He gave them food and brought them in close, even knowing what they had done to him. This was a man of destiny.

YOUR THOUGHTS BECOME YOUR DESTINY

The thoughts you dwell upon will become your reality, whether they are true or false. Too often people worry unnecessarily and live unhappy lives because of their limited thinking. As a man thinks, so is he. You will never live right by thinking wrong. What you see today is the result of the thoughts that have permeated your mind. Your life today is the result of your thinking.

I have witnessed the aftermath of those who have focused on wrong thinking. When we see a friend or acquaintance who is quiet and does not have much to say, automatically we begin to think negative thoughts and wonder what is wrong. More often than not, there is nothing wrong—only a negative perception that we are allowing into our thoughts.

One day someone told Sharon about a situation they were facing. I was never made privy to this conversation, but the next time I saw this person I was preoccupied with many things. My silence had nothing to do with this person. Even though I was completely innocent of the knowledge of this individual's conversation with my wife, my quiet demeanor that day cast a different perception upon them. They began thinking I was withdrawing from them because they thought Sharon had informed me of their conversation. The fact was I knew nothing about their conversation with my wife.

Eventually, this person came and said to me, "I know you are bothered with me because of what I told your wife."

I said, "Excuse me; I do not know what you are talking about."

They began to expound to me about the conversation they had had with Sharon. They took it for granted she had told me about their conversation; their perception became their reality and almost ended our friendship.

YOUR SUBCONSCIOUS AFFECTS YOUR THOUGHTS

The main difference between the conscious and the subconscious mind lies in their basic functions. The conscious mind is responsible for rationalization and logical thinking, and the subconscious mind is responsible for involuntary actions. The conscious mind encompasses the thoughts we are aware of at any given moment. The subconscious makes decisions without our needing to actively think about them.

I believe past feelings and experiences are stored within the confines of your subconscious existence. Positive or negative thoughts that have perpetually pummeled your mind eventually become a fixture in this part of your mind. Memories stored there include habits, fears, abuses, rejection, failures, insecurities, low self-esteem, anger, bad decisions, beliefs, desires, and good and bad memories. When you face something fearful, painful, or traumatic in the present, your mind draws from this inventory of days gone by and summons up either good or bad feelings. When this happens, your subconscious overrides your conscious mind. If negative memories take over, you may make irrational choices. You may become fearful, even panic. You may say words that harm someone you love. You could even lose a relationship or a marriage. Rage may gain control of your actions.

Because of this danger, you need to put good things in your conscious mind all the time. What goes in becomes part of your subconscious and eventually comes out. If you continue to put good things in, they will gradually help root out the old negative memories that have been there a long time.

Overriding years of painful and fearful experiences doesn't happen quickly. It takes intentional effort to store the good things. This involves a daily and perpetual process of renewing your mind about who you are in Christ, especially when something negative comes up. Right then is the time to replace the bad thought with a good one—don't allow a bad thought to stay and fester. Instead, replace it with something positive immediately.

Your memories won't disappear, but you can prevent bad memories from controlling your future. Over time, you can change them from being painful as you apply the principles in this book.

If you always think gloomy thoughts, daily experiences will seem bad. However, if you change your thinking and become a cheerful person, you can handle the negative things coming to you in a positive way. Second Corinthians 10:4–5 reveals how we can change bad thoughts and images into good ones and live a life of peace so we can think ourselves happy, no matter what the circumstance may be.

*For the weapons of our warfare are not carnal
but mighty in God for pulling down
strongholds, casting down arguments and
every high thing that exalts itself against the
knowledge of God, bringing every thought
into captivity to the obedience of Christ.*

NEGATIVE THOUGHTS CREATE NEGATIVE FEELINGS

Negative thoughts create negative feelings, which will ultimately keep you from being happy and enjoying life. Allowing negative thoughts and feelings to remain is, in essence, bringing a death sentence to your future joy. You will never rise above and will always remain a slave to negativity unless you face this foe and give it no place in your life. Remove your negative thoughts today, and embrace your future.

If you continue to allow negative and disempowering thoughts to have a place in your life, they will soon be ingrained in your subconscious mind, thus birthing feelings and emotions that will take you farther down the road of despair. Continuing to take such a position, you will find yourself gazing from a distance at the good things your Father has planned for you, while the distance between your present situation and the Father's planned destination grows even wider.

CONTROL YOUR FEELINGS OR THEY WILL CONTROL YOU

Have you ever been at work and received a message that your supervisor wanted to meet with you? Likely your first thought was, *I wonder what is wrong.* A quick inventory of your mind searched the happenstances of the last couple of weeks, frantically trying to discover what negative action you must have taken to merit the supervisor's request for a meeting.

Someone may have called you and left a brief message saying they need to speak with you, and you suddenly find yourself wondering what is wrong. Frantic thoughts crowd your mind; peace is nowhere to be found. Worry and mayhem take the V.I.P. seat in your mind's *priority seating section* merely because someone left you a message that they wanted to speak to you.

The perception of an optimistic, positive person, one who has happy thoughts permeating his being, is different when he receives a message that the boss wants to see him. A sense of excitement exudes from his persona, as he expects good news, perhaps a promotion or possibly special appreciation for a job well done. Fear holds no rank because he lives with the confidence and expectations that good things await him.

Which scenario better describes your reaction to situations like this? Do you quiver behind the intimidation of fear, or are you the one who lives with a sense of excitement because you know something good is about to happen to you? Your inner thinking process is important to your well-being. What you *think on* becomes your reality. Happiness and joy in life begin with your thinking.

As a born-again Christian, you have the Word of God to help develop you in your thought process. In every situation and in every circumstance, you can be in control of your thinking. You may not be in control of the situation; however, you can control your role and your reaction to what confronts you. If you choose to interpret things in a good and positive light, trusting God for the outcome, you will remain happy.

Do not conform to this world and its thought process, but rather be transformed into a new person by the way you think.

> *Don't copy the behavior and customs of this*
> *world, but let God transform you into a new*
> *person by changing the way you think. Then*
> *you will learn to know God's will for you,*
> *which is good and pleasing and perfect.*
> ROMANS 12:2 NLT

Man is a three-part being: he is a spirit, he has a soul, and he lives in a body. When you are born again, the Holy Spirit becomes alive in your human spirit, and you receive illumination and light from Him. You are a new creation in your spirit.

Your soul is your will, mind, and emotions. Your body is made up of your five senses. It is your soul that needs the renewing process, and this is something you must continually do. When you become a follower of Christ, you are charged to renew your mind. The renewing of your mind is your responsibility. You must become a responsible manager of your thought life and, in doing so, prepare yourself to walk in His glory.

As a believer, you have great power available to you through His Spirit. I cannot express this any more clearly—you *must* renew your mind, surround yourself with positive people, immerse yourself in His Word, and *think on these things*.

CHOOSE TO WALK BY FAITH

What painful experiences have you had in life? Have you suffered from a failed relationship? Have you lost a good job? Have you been rejected by someone you loved? Have you been passed over for something you desperately wanted? When that event occurred in your life, how did it make you feel? What did you think at the time? How did you respond to the situation? Did you complain and get discouraged? Did you doubt God? Did you allow the experience to change you negatively?

I hope not. I hope you thought good thoughts and gave God praise during the ordeal. But if not, you can still redeem that failure by allowing it to motivate you to react differently in the future. Your negative thoughts didn't improve the situation, did they? They actually made the situation worse. When bad experiences come your way (remember, Jesus promised they would in John 16:33), you have no choice but to endure them. Whether you want to or not, you have to navigate the storms of life. But you can derive benefit from those storms if you choose to walk through them in faith, not defeat.

WHOSE VOICE ARE YOU LISTENING TO?

Each of us has a say in what voices we listen to. There is danger in listening to the voice of a stranger. Jesus said, "My sheep hear my voice, and I know them, and they follow Me" (John 10:27). There is a voice of darkness, a voice of reason, a voice from the past, a voice of the present, and the voice of God. Which voice will you listen to? Which voice will you allow to be established in your life? I want to encourage you to hear His voice and be found in the presence of happiness.

An old Cherokee Indian was teaching his grandson about life. "An inner conflict rages," he said to the boy. "There is a battle between two wolves. One wolf is evil: this wolf is filled with envy, sorrow, regret, greed, arrogance, self-pity, resentment, inferiority, lies, pride, superiority, and ego. The second wolf is good: this wolf is filled with joy, happiness, love, peace, hope, serenity, humility, kindness, benevolence, empathy, compassion, truth, faith, and generosity."

The young lad thought about this for a moment and then asked his grandfather, "Which wolf will win?"

The Cherokee chief replied, "The one you feed." The same fight is going on inside you and those around you. What thoughts are you feeding?

Let me share with you how I feed myself with good thoughts. I start every day by giving thanks to God, praying, and reading my Bible. I read through the Bible every year and have for many years. The Scriptures always bring great comfort. Praying for my thought process helps me keep my emotions under control in any circumstance.

The Bible tells us to put on the whole armor of God. I believe this should be a daily process. These scriptures tell us we are fighting not just against people but also against satanic spirit beings in the unseen world, which are very evil, warring against us. They continually try to get us to think wrong things. I do my best to put on that armor of God daily.

> *Put on all of God's armor so that you will*
> *be able to stand firm against all strategies*
> *of the devil. For we are not fighting against*
> *flesh-and-blood enemies, but against evil*
> *rulers and authorities of the unseen world,*
> *against mighty powers in this dark world, and*
> *against evil spirits in the heavenly places.*

> *Therefore, put on every piece of God's armor*
> *so you will be able to resist the enemy in the*
> *time of evil. Then after the battle you will still*
> *be standing firm. Stand your ground, putting on*
> *the belt of truth and the body armor of God's*
> *righteousness. For shoes, put on the peace that*
> *comes from the Good News so that you will be*
> *fully prepared. In addition to all of these, hold up*
> *the shield of faith to stop the fiery arrows of the*
> *devil. Put on salvation as your helmet, and take*
> *the sword of the Spirit, which is the word of God.*
> EPHESIANS 6:11–18 NLT

I start by touching my head and asking God to help me with my thinking throughout the day. "God, help me to be aware when I am confronted by an evil spirit and not react improperly if someone says or does something to me, or if something uncomfortable or unexpected happens to me."

I touch my ears and ask God to help me to listen not to negative voices but only to the good voices that will lead me in the right direction. I touch my eyes and ask God to help me see what I believe instead of believing what I see. I pray, "Lord, let me see with eyes of faith instead of doubt and fear."

Then I touch my lips, and I pray for God to help me with my words so I will speak and say words of faith and things that will be helpful to me and to others and will glorify God. "Take control of what I say, O LORD, and guard my lips" (Psalm 141:3 NLT).

Finally, I put my hand on my heart and ask God to help me love and have compassion for everyone throughout the day. I ask Him to help me be aware of keeping the shield of faith up so the fiery darts that come will not get inside me. I declare, "I will walk by faith and not by sight and feelings."

Start your day by feeding yourself with good thoughts, and throughout the day remind yourself of who you are in Christ.

GOD'S PURPOSE FOR YOUR LIFE

You are a child of God, and He has a purpose for your life. Don't allow your circumstances to limit what is possible for all your tomorrows. Never allow your present situation to have the final say. Your current circumstances are not your final destination. Don't allow your feelings to control you. They are swayed by too many foreign forces, as well as voices that have no foundation based upon His Word. If they refuse to coincide with His Word of Truth, dismiss them from your mind. You must create your happiness in Jesus—and that is the end of the story.

Lining your thoughts up with God's Word allows you to focus on His purpose for your life. Intentionally pursuing His purpose brings a depth of happiness few find. When happiness in Him is firm, and the joy of the Lord is your strength, you are positioned to fulfill His *purpose* in your life. It has been said that the two greatest days of your life are the day you were born and the day you discover why.

Herein lies your ultimate fulfillment.

Life happenings can suck you in and thwart the promises of your future, often bringing great destruction. It is time to remove the cancers that are trying to annihilate your future. *Purpose* must dictate your decisions in relationships, in your endeavors, and on your path. If *His purpose* is not at the helm of your resolutions in life, then you must relinquish those resolutions and commit to His plan. Your most passionate goal should be to fulfill His purpose in your life.

God's purpose for your life predates your conception. You get to make many choices, so make them with His purpose for your life in mind. He planned it before your first breath, even before your existence. Your input was not required; your consultation was not sought. When you were born, you looked like your parents. *When you die, you will look like your decisions.*

Choose to harness your hopes, dreams, aspirations, goals, and life to His promises. Choose to reject toxic thoughts of fear or timidity. Dismiss any notion of mediocrity or lack. Vehemently deny the right for darkness to set up camp anywhere near your province. Refuse to be defined by past mistakes, limited by cynics, or conformed to the status quo. Believing unscriptural statements about yourself or anything else is self-defeating and leads you away from God's purpose for your life.

Choose life by receiving Jesus. Accept the covenant promises afforded to you because of this choice and fervent belief. Embrace the dawning of this new day and this new chapter in life. Dream big—for He is big!

Some people in your circle may not be in your corner. Don't compromise your faith in an unwise relationship. There are relationships for a reason and relationships for a season. Your faith is at the heart of every relationship, and you cannot afford to compromise it. If people can't grow with us, they cannot go with us.

My friend, your present situation is *not* your final destination. His purpose is clear. His voice prevails as truth. You are not dead, so God is not done. You get to write the next chapter of your life. *Make it epic!* If you run after your destiny, you are certain to escape your history. We all have had some form of brokenness, but the last time I checked, broken crayons can still make beautiful pictures.

If the enemy can distract you, he can mute your influence. When God's purpose becomes foremost in your focus, you can be sure the enemy will throw distractions in your path. Some distractions may be good things in themselves but become destructive if they deter you from God's priorities and plans. Busyness. People's invitations or demands. Even serving in the church. When they become distractions, they eclipse our God-given aspirations to be all the Almighty has called us to be. While they may be honorable, some *good* things may not be the *God things* for your life.

Beware of dream thieves. Well-meaning friends, even family members, can be the biggest distraction in your pursuit of purpose. Dream thieves often come dressed in church clothes. While they may be well-meaning, too often they persuade you to place other things before your God-given purpose in life. And remember this: there is more to your life than the current path you are on.

ALWAYS PUT GOD FIRST

But seek first the kingdom of God
and His righteousness, and all these
things shall be added to you.
MATTHEW 6:33

One of the most precious things I have learned is to put God first no matter what is going on in my life. It's easy to read or quote this scripture, but if you want to be happy, this is a part of your foundation of happiness. Seek to put God first.

As you grow in spiritual maturity and insight, you will begin to recognize when your focus is being invaded. As you walk closely with Him, you will have the foresight to see distractions that lie in wait, scheming their next move. There is an enemy called *average*. God's plan for your life is not average, mediocre, plain, paltry, or mundane. He wants to take you into the Promised Land. Don't let fear, anxiety, worry, self-doubt, discontentment, unforgiveness, grief—or any other negative thought patterns—keep you from God's purpose for your life or the abundant life He wants to give you.

Walk with Jesus . . . trust His Word . . . and think yourself happy!

www.ingramcontent.com/pod-product-compliance
Lightning Source LLC
La Vergne TN
LVHW051240080426
835513LV00016B/1693